The View from the Centre

KEITH EYEONS

Ellis &
Maultby

Ellis and Maultby
Cambridge
England
enquiries@ellisandmaultby.co.uk

ISBNs
978-1-9997631-3-8 (ebook)
978-1-9997631-4-5 (paperback)
978-1-9997631-5-2 (hardback)

It hath been the wisdom of the Church of *England*,
ever since the first compiling of her Publick Liturgy,
to keep the Mean between the two Extreams.

From the Preface to the 1662 edition of the *Book of Common Prayer*

Contents

Chapter One
Finding the Centre

INTRODUCTION

Why are churches so different? Some Christians worship in total silence, while others cheer and shout and dance. Some clergy lead services by chatting informally into microphones like TV presenters, while others chant solemnly in Latin. Some church buildings are covered with golden mosaics or gothic pinnacles, while others have beige carpets and plain magnolia walls. Some have communion every day, while others share the bread and wine only once or twice a year. Some place great emphasis on sermons which last an hour, while others have occasional homilies of only a few minutes. Some are keen to bless same-sex marriages, while others denounce homosexuality as an abomination. Some have only male clergy, while others celebrate the ministry of women. Some congregations are entirely independent, while others include prayers in every service for higher authorities such as the diocesan bishop, the Queen or the Pope.

I started exploring Christianity as a young adult, having been brought up as an atheist, and found much of this complexity intriguing but baffling. Christians, on the whole, were not much help, preferring to mutter darkly about the errors and absurdities of the other groups. They dismissed others as unsound, or happy clappy, or obsessed with manmade rituals, or lacking in valid sacraments, or fanatical, or just not really Christian at all. I found that church names revealed little to the uninformed visitor, and it could be a struggle to know why the same town might include a Parish Church of St. Botolph, a Cornerstone Christian Fellowship, an Emmanuel United Reformed Church and a Church of Our Lady of Lourdes. As a newcomer, I found it difficult to see why these churches functioned separately, or to understand what sort of relationships they might have with each other.

Nevertheless, my journey was a fascinating one which led me to appreciate many different approaches to Christianity, and to sympathise with various contrasting perspectives that had been adopted by believers in good faith. It also led me to find a lasting home in a place which seemed to me to be somewhere in the midst of it all, the middle ground of the Church of England.

This book therefore serves two purposes. The first purpose is to provide a way for people to find their bearings amidst the diversity of Christian faith and spirituality. The book offers a map to help understand the experience of God around the global Church in its many forms: Catholic and Protestant, traditionalist and progressive. It assesses the main issues which have divided Christians in the past, and the controversies which cause the greatest tensions today.

By pulling together these different perspectives, it follows on from my first book *The Theology of Everything*. There I argued that Christian theology can bring together the data from all our various faculties: our physical senses, our ability to make scientific measurements, and our awareness of beauty, meaning, goodness, and our experiences of love, community and prayer. Now I continue to try to pay attention to a broad range of data by looking at the various branches of the world's largest faith, while also exploring more deeply the inner workings of theology.

The second purpose of the book is then to argue for a meaningful central vantage point from which all the main approaches to Christianity can be understood and appreciated. It suggests a way of drawing on the best of all of these various traditions, while diagnosing and rejecting their main problems. And it claims that a convenient place to see this kind of perspective is from the middle ground of the Church of England.

If you are familiar with middle-of-the-road Anglicanism, my claim may sound surprisingly ambitious and uncharacteristically arrogant. Those of us who rejoice to be in the central regions of a broad church are usually quite vague about what we actually think. We position ourselves politely somewhere between the extreme points of view which are being loudly articulated by our more strident neighbours. Rowan Williams has declared that 'reticence' is one of the defining features of Anglicanism, and I would add that its middle ground is traditionally the most reticent of all.

But I think that this is a time when the centre urgently needs to be renewed, celebrated and clearly-signposted, both in the life of the Church and in many contemporary social and political issues. In today's world, extreme points of view are heard much more clearly than voices of moderation. We have always had our natural tribal instincts, but these are now reinforced within our social media bubbles. Twitter-storms and lazy forms of journalism often give a platform for opposing zealots to shout at each other and to react in outrage. Identifying and valuing a middle ground with a more thoughtful perspective is an urgent task.

MY STORY: SEARCHING FOR THE CENTRE

My life and my experiences have shaped the perspective I have formed, and so I think it is relevant to describe how I reached my point of view. In *The Theology of Everything*, I wrote about the vivid experience of God which shattered the atheism of my childhood. People who know me now often assume that such a clear divine shove must have propelled me immediately towards church membership and then confidently on towards ordination in the Church of England. But I found plenty to be confused about, and I had no idea how I should find a place within the complex landscape of religious belief.

My family did not believe in God and were active members of the local Humanist group, so the only religious aspect to my upbring-ing had been the Church of England primary school which I attended because it was a conveniently short walk from my home. I was happy there, but the teaching of Christianity seemed to me to be dull, mostly lacking in conviction, and disconnected from any of the things which were more evidently true. The two activities I enjoyed most at that school were mathematics and music, so I did acquire a love for the hymn tunes which I played on my tenor recorder during the daily assemblies. I was persuaded to join the choir at the parish church for a short time, but I found it an overwhelmingly strange experience. There were rituals which I found bizarre and vaguely sinister, like wearing robes and bowing in front of a large table. Nobody explained why we did such things, and it was made all the more surreal by the fact that everyone around me just seemed mildly bored.

I felt very sure about a lot of things at the age of eleven, one of which was that the Church of England would have no further role in my life. Computers, space travel and flute-playing were my top three interests at that time. My secondary school was mostly a refreshingly secular experience, but I did a lot more singing there, and the choir's concert repertoire borrowed often from the Western classical traditions of amazingly beautiful sacred music. An appreciation of a religious sense of beauty began to find its way into my soul without me identifying it as such.

When my great spiritual awakening happened at the age of 18, it connected with the usual teenage ability to feel things with extraordinary intensity and to assume that all nearby adults are completely missing the point. It seemed obvious to me that my own deeply authentic mysticism had nothing to do with the local church of the mildly bored, just as it had nothing to do with my parents' Humanism.

So I was much more interested in Eastern religions to begin with, reading eagerly about meditation and altered states of consciousness. But I was surprised to find also a growing sense of being drawn towards Christianity. I looked seriously at the teachings of Jesus for the first time, and was startled by how radical and pacifist they seemed. The first religious group I very nervously connected with was the Quakers, whose simple form of silent worship was far closer to my own experiences than anything involving rituals, liturgies or sermons.

This was the time when I arrived as an undergraduate in Cambridge, a city full of Christian heritage and with much for me to explore. To my delight, I was able to form new friendships with others who enjoyed talking about the meaning of life. I trusted my contemporaries, and it was a great joy to find others who could speak with great enthusiasm about the importance of God in their lives.

Among religious students, Evangelical Christianity was then by far the dominant force, and so I began a rather turbulent relationship with that tradition. My new Evangelical friends were passionate about their faith, eager to talk about it, and shared an enviably strong sense of community with each other. I admired their enthusiasm, seeing something authentic in them which resembled my own strong desire to find a way of shaping my life around my experiences of God. They clearly found joy and delight in their prayer and worship, were inspired by an awareness of divine love, shared a warm and quirky sense of humour, enjoyed very close friendships, and sometimes said things about a personal relationship with God that I found very appealing.

But at other times they talked about God in terms which made him sound to me like a grumpy and distant bureaucrat. I was puzzled when they talked about the pointlessness of all human attempts to be good, and about salvation in terms of a transfer of divine wrath from us onto Jesus. Nevertheless, their patient attempts to explain themselves led to me taking a step of faith at an evangelistic talk given by the Cambridge Inter-Collegiate Christian Union. The speaker explained the first chapter of Paul's Letter to the Colossians, which describes Jesus as the image of the invisible God, the one in whom all things hold together, the one who came to bring reconciliation between God and the whole cosmos. I prayed the prayer of repentance, faith and commitment which he invited us to pray at the end, and from that evening have considered myself to be a Christian.

My conversion brought a great sense of joy and a feeling of coming home. It cemented a set of very supportive and deep friendships, and gave me a new set of resources and routines to help me weave my spirituality into my whole life. But it was painfully difficult to explain to my shocked and baffled parents, and it brought many, many more questions.

From the very beginning, I was always exploring at least two highly contrasting forms of Christianity. At first, it was the Quakers and the Christian Union. The Quakers emphasised the need for authentic spiritual experience, while the Christian Union emphasised

the sound doctrine found in the Bible. The Quakers emphasised ethical and political activism, while the Christian Union said that human
works would never save us. The Quakers believed in sexual equality
and took a kindly and affirming approach to homosexuality, while
the Christian Union insisted on having a male president and said that
any sex outside the marriage of a man and a woman was sinful. The
Quakers worshipped in stillness and silence, while the Christian Union
sang noisy and enthusiastic worship songs proclaiming our faith. The
Quakers waited for people to come to find them, while the Christian
Union expended huge energy in trying to invite people in. And the
Quakers said that the Spirit of God was at work in all people, while
the Christian Union said that only those with the right kind of faith in
Jesus could ever know God.

There was almost no overlap between the two approaches, and yet
they each meant something profound to me which I felt was connected.
My Quaker friends thought that the Evangelicals in the Christian Union
were narrow-minded and excessively dogmatic, and my Christian
Union friends thought that the Quakers were obviously wrong and
needed to be saved. Meanwhile, I thought that the Evangelicals were
missing out on the spiritual treasures of silent prayer, and that the
Quakers were missing out on the very positive and confident appreciation of Jesus Christ enjoyed by those who spent more time reading
the Bible.

For a while, I struggled to know which approach to prioritise. Was
I primarily a meditative, spiritual person, exploring a set of mystical
experiences which went beyond all words and would be recognised
by people of many faiths? Or was I primarily a Christian believer who
happened to love silent prayer? I found that the Quakers were worryingly divided about what they believed and unsure whether they were
still a Christian denomination or not, so a search for more clarity led
to the conclusion that my future lay elsewhere.

Where, though, was very difficult to say. My Evangelical friends
went to various different churches in central Cambridge on Sundays,
and there were lots of other ones which they disapproved of or simply

knew nothing about. I bought a book called *Why All These Denominations?*[1] at that time, and visited various different ones in an attempt to make some sense of it all. In the end, back home for the summer vacation, I joined a church which was a joint Baptist and United Reformed Church (itself an amalgamation of the former Congregationalist and Presbyterian denominations). It was a very welcoming fellowship of wise and friendly people, offering a gentler, broader experience of Protestantism than the student Evangelicalism I had known. The minister was generous with his time, answering my questions and leading me through a very helpful course. I was baptised by full immersion, which was one of the most meaningful and profound experiences of my life. I felt happy and at peace there.

Back in Cambridge for my second year, there was plenty more for me to explore and to think about. The Christian Union had also given me the task of recording all the talks at their central university meetings. I think they thought this was a good way of holding my attention and stopping me going off the rails. Each Saturday, a distinguished visiting Evangelical speaker would address us, expounding a Bible passage for 40 minutes or so. I therefore was responsible for looking after an archive of about 600 sermons on audio cassettes stored in a large box in my room.

By this time, I was becoming very aware of the greatest division among the Evangelical students of that time. A significant minority were Charismatics, and the rest were either worried or confused about them. To be Charismatic meant emphasising the miraculous role of the Holy Spirit in the Christian life, expecting to experience God powerfully and to develop spiritual gifts. Charismatics enjoyed speaking and singing in tongues: spontaneously using random-sounding words in worship which conveyed great depths of emotion. They expected God to speak in the present day through prophesies and words of knowledge, alongside their preaching from the Bible. Their style of worship was full of passion and energy, with hands raised in adoration, and sustained times of singing as one song flowed into another.

---

1   By Gilbert W Kirby (1988) *Why All These Denominations? A History of the Church in Britain* Kingsway – a clear and wide-ranging account from a charismatic Evangelical perspective

The other Evangelicals believed that the Holy Spirit had written the Bible and, with that great task completed long ago, now had no further comment to make. Their services emphasised the importance of understanding the Scriptures. They were deeply suspicious of anything experiential or emotional, and thought that feelings were often misleading. They said that being a Christian was about knowing the truth of the Gospel. Singing was not an expression of the heart towards God, but a way of using words to proclaim the doctrines of Christianity. And prayer was always about our mission to explain the faith to our friends.

Having been jolted into faith by a set of religious experiences, it was obvious that my sympathies would lie with the Charismatics. And so I joined a daily Charismatic prayer group with great enthusiasm, and found there a set of powerful experiences which fed my hunger for an encounter with God which was shared with others. This was the most intense form of human community which I have ever encountered. There were tears and hugs and much laughter. We read the Bible and debated what it meant for us today. We started to feel that God was speaking directly to our group. We tried to help some of the homeless people we saw around us. And we developed a rather grandiose and triumphant sense of our own significance as part of a great divine work.

Alongside that, something else happened, whose significance only became clear to me gradually. I started going to my college chapel, which had daily services led by two Church of England clergy, a male dean and a female chaplain. This was my first experience of worshipping as a Christian in a more traditional setting. I still had the strong aversion to religious rituals which I had acquired as a child. Getting baptised had been a challenge to that mindset, but I had chosen to join a church with modern furnishings and a general lack of ceremony. My college chapel had pews, stained glass and an elaborately decorated interior, within which worship often involved 16th-century English or occasional Latin. Nevertheless, it turned out to be remarkably easy to settle in there. There was a famous and excellent choir, some of whom were students on same course as me or were familiar from the social life of the college. And the dean and chaplain, despite being dressed in grand and formal robes, were warm, welcoming, and very good at explaining things and helping newcomers to feel at home.

I remember going to a weekday Choral Evensong towards the end of my first year, at a time when I was troubled by the way that the Quakers were arguing about what they now believed. Choral Evensong unfolded gently around me with its traditional language and stately harmonies, just as it had done for centuries, with no fuss, with amazing beauty, with a deep sense of unhurried calm. It felt like strolling through mountain scenery, surrounded by something reassuring and majestic that was far more enduring than the worries of the day.

But it was the Communion services which most captured my heart. I settled into a routine of going every Sunday and Wednesday morning, and found something amazingly powerful about the experience of meeting Jesus in the blessing, breaking and sharing of bread and wine. This was stiller and deeper than my Charismatic enthusiasms, and felt more real than all the deductions of my over-active brain. God was there, in that sacred space, for me to meet in a liturgy which was shared with Christians from many centuries and many countries. I soon grew to love the words, and to find more and more meaning in them as they became part of me.

During my second year, I became a chapel warden, one of the team of students who helped in the running of the Chapel. I found a deep joy in setting up the Chapel for services, carefully placing the silver and the linen on the altar, seeing a divine beauty in all the little details. I owe a great debt to the dean and the chaplain, who came from different backgrounds within the Church of England and gave me a gentle introduction to a much wider world of Christian thought and spirituality.

I also, to my surprise, began to develop an interest in the Roman Catholic Church. I was trying to find books about meditative prayer and Christian mysticism, and most of the ones I came across were written by Catholics. I started to discover the rich traditions of contemplative prayer explored by centuries of monks and nuns. The elaborate world of Catholic liturgy and doctrine was very different from the simplicity I had found among the Quakers, but those Catholic writers talked about the encounter with God in stillness and silence in ways which I found

very inspiring. And they often linked that contemplative spirituality
with the experience of the Mass, which connected with my love of Communion services in the Chapel. One of my most inspiring experiences
as a student was going to a series of talks given by a sister from the
Institute of the Blessed Virgin Mary, who talked very warmly about
prayer as getting to know God.

Something deep and lasting was taking root there, an experience of
sacrament, liturgy, tradition and contemplation which would grow and
become a source of spiritual nourishment over decades. Nevertheless,
at the time, my attention was primarily on my involvement in student
Evangelical Christianity, where I found much to excite me, and much
that was troubling. At the end of my second year, I was put in charge
of one of the Christian Union's Bible study groups. But as time went
by, and as I got to know the Bible more and more, I got increasingly
sceptical about Evangelicalism.

The Christian Union proclaimed that the Bible was the infallible
and authoritative Word of God. I had caught their enthusiasm for it,
and so had read all of it in a year. And, far from confirming a clear
sense of Evangelical doctrine, reading the Bible left me more and more
puzzled by them. Why did Evangelicals never talk about the Kingdom
of God, despite it being the main theme of Jesus' teaching in three of
the four Gospels? Why did they say so much about initial conversion
and sound doctrine, and so little about the moral and social themes
which filled much of the Bible? Why did they insist that God could only
forgive sin if he found someone else to punish, despite the fact that the
Bible never actually said that? Why did they omit the Deuterocanon-
ical books which Catholics included? Where could one actually find a
divinely-given statement of which books were meant to be in there?
Why did the books of the Bible never actually talk about the Bible as a
thing? Why were Evangelical students so enthusiastic about proclaiming the infallibility of the Bible when most of them had not even read
all of it? And how could they be so calm about all the disturbing parts
of the Old Testament? I began to note how selective they were in their
favourite verses. Time after time, people would quote individual verses

from St Paul's Letter to the Romans, with occasionally visits to Isaiah 53 and John 14.6. They paid very little attention to the surrounding context.

When our female college chaplain was lamenting the fact that the Church of England would not yet allow women to be priests, I remember one Christian Union leader pulling out a pocket New Testament and very efficiently quoting one verse which he thought decisively established a ban on women in leadership until the end of time. I also noticed that Evangelicals were saying things condemning gay relationships which placed a heavy weight on a few words spoken in a very different kind of society from our own. The Bible did not seem to me to address the possibility of a loving and faithful same-sex relationship, either positively or negatively.

Meanwhile, I got increasingly bored by the fact that most of the talks I heard, whichever Bible text they expounded, seemed to conclude from that passage that it was our job to tell our friends that Jesus died to take the punishment for our sins so that we can go to heaven when we die. There was surprisingly little interest in spiritual growth, due to a constant emphasis on conversion as the only thing that mattered. In all these ways, Evangelicals seemed to me to be not taking the Bible very seriously.

The Christian Union was careful to focus on what it saw as the central message of the Gospel, and to preserve it from anything else which might marginalise or undermine it. Unlike their American counterparts, those English Evangelicals had very little to say about politics. I found also that they were mostly quite detached from anything to do with science, ethics, art, poetry, literature or other areas of wider human interest and activity. And they had a strong tendency to ignore most of the 20 centuries of Christian history, as if the Bible were connected immediately to the present day. Full of questions about how all these things might fit together, I moved on from learning about physics and spent my final year as an undergraduate studying the history and philosophy of science. As I explored the history of Western thought, I was fascinated to see some of the many ways in which Christianity in various forms was woven through it.

Despite my sense of exasperation with the narrowness of much Evangelicalism, I was very aware that the people around me of my generation who were enthusiastic about their faith were mostly Evangelicals. Their love for each other and for God was very evident, as was the importance they attributed to prayer and to learning from the Scriptures. And so I still felt more at home among them than anywhere else. I was often quite dismissive of the college chapel, and quite hesitant for much of the time about exploring the interest I had found in Catholic spirituality.

Meanwhile, a sense of calling to Christian ministry had been developing, and there were lots of things that I wanted to learn about people and the work of God in the world. I therefore applied to an Evangelical charity which sent young adults to serve as volunteers in local churches. And they sent me to a village in Warwickshire, to work in a Church of England parish church which had a clearly-stated Evangelical character.

Of all the years in my life, that is probably the one I remember in the most detail. It did me a huge amount of good. I spent a lot of time doing ordinary works of Christian service: visiting the elderly and the bereaved, printing posters, putting out chairs for meetings, playing keyboard and flute in services, leading a Sunday School class, helping to run a youth group, and getting better at relating to other people. It was hard work, and much of it was very good fun and highly rewarding. The church community was warm, friendly, encouraging and appreciative, and the vicar was a very inspiring teacher. It was remarkably active for a village church, especially in its work with children and teenagers, running four different groups for various age ranges. The lively style of the church connected well with the children's sense of fun and with the idealism of the teenagers and their need for supportive friendships.

I found much to admire there and to learn from. But it was an isolated place with poor public transport links, and there was no way to get to and from any of my Cambridge friends within the one day off I had each week. I was preoccupied with too many fascinating and troublesome questions, which I did not feel I could talk about. The Evangelical approach was to say that we simply needed to have faith in Jesus and to believe in the authority of the Bible. But I kept

on noticing that people were fitting their reading of the Bible into a
theological framework which was not itself set out in the Bible. They
would confidently say, for example, that God has to punish all sins, or
that we can go to heaven when we die, or that the Bible is infallible,
or that God is outside time, none of which are ideas stated directly in
the Scriptures. They had a way of highlighting particular verses and
of interpreting them to fit their theological framework. Evangelicals, I
concluded, had a tradition, a way of reading the Bible which was carefully passed on through sermons and worship songs, and expounded
in books and doctrinal statements. But they disapproved of tradition
and thought that they were avoiding it, sincerely believing that they
were just reading the Bible.

I could not see any way round this odd contradiction, and therefore
suddenly found myself looking in a surprising direction. I was aware
that the world's largest Church had a confidently-stated set of traditions which they believed were inspired by God. The Roman Catholic
Church is very open about believing both in the Bible and in a particular
way of reading it. To me, they seemed to resemble the Charismatic
Evangelicals in believing in the continuing work of the Holy Spirit. But,
whereas Charismatics tended to dismiss 20 centuries of history and to
focus on exciting present-day experiences, the Catholics could tell a
joined-up story of God's work through the whole history of the Church.

I had absorbed a lot of hostility to Catholicism from my parents and
from the Evangelical world, and so this felt like a disturbing direction
to be looking in, and something of a betrayal of those who had guided
me. But I started reading Catholic theology, and found great delight in
what I discovered. There was a far deeper engagement with philosophy
than I had found among any Christians before, a far greater clarity of
thought and breadth of vision about the whole nature of truth. It was
like emerging from under water and taking great gulps of fresh air at
last.

A book by Aidan Nichols on *The Shape of Catholic Theology*[2] was
especially intriguing. I loved the idea that theology might have a shape,
a meaningful structure, and a set of harmonious relationships with all

2   Aidan Nichols O.P. (1991) *The Shape of Catholic Theology* T & T Clark

truth. That sounded much more promising than the evangelistic slogans that I usually kept hearing. Catholics, I discovered, could engage very thoughtfully with philosophy as well as having that love of contemplative prayer which I had already noticed and admired.

My journey of exploration of Christian churches was by now pulling me in several directions. Firstly, I was a member of a Baptist and United Reformed church at home that was a gentle and moderate form of Protestantism. Secondly, I was working in an Evangelical parish in the Church of England. Thirdly, I had got into the habit of walking to the next village every Wednesday morning, where the high Anglican parish church was much more Catholic in style and offered a midweek Communion service. Fourthly, I was reading books of Roman Catholic theology and starting to explore the practice of asking for the prayers of the Blessed Virgin Mary and all the saints. Alongside all of that, I was pondering a sense of call to ordination, while still being unsure which Christian denomination I was supposed to be in. It was a lot to process all at once.

I found much to attract me in Catholicism, but also much that I was unsure about. Working in a church had turned out to be a surprisingly lonely experience at times, and the requirement for Catholic priests to be permanently single now seemed very challenging. I also struggled with the idea that the Catholic Church could be infallible, just as I had struggled with the idea that the Bible could be infallible. I could not see that anything outside the perfect logic of mathematics could ever be truly infallible, and the Catholic Church seemed to have amassed quite a large number of dubious ideas over the centuries, from the sale of indulgences to the ban on contraception.

Nearly all Roman Catholics have grown up in that denomination, and most of them seem cheerfully and openly to distance themselves from significant parts of its doctrines and practices, but I found out that anyone joining from the outside is required to promise that they believe everything that the Catholic Church teaches. This seemed to me to be an incredibly high barrier to entry, and one that I could not imagine ever climbing over.

Two conclusions emerged from that year. Firstly, I soon realised that I was far too confused to seek ordination in any church at that time. I built instead on the experiences of that year by going back home to London to train to be a teacher. Secondly, I decided to take some time in London to explore the Anglo-Catholicism which is widely found there: this is the high-church tradition in the Church of England which has restored many of the Catholic traditions of worship and spirituality abandoned at the Reformation.

I spent two years in London on a part-time teaching course which was combined with working in a Church of England school in a trou-bled inner-city area. The school was associated with a very interesting parish church, which had been closed down for some years, but had recently been redeveloped as a joint community centre and space for worship. The sides of the building had been partitioned into meeting rooms, a kitchen and toilets, while the central part of the nave had been left as a big space which could be used in lots of different ways. Many different community groups met there during the week, so that the church was active in serving the local area in many ways. Then there was an altar on wheels which we brought out on Sundays, along with rows of chairs.

There were many aspects of Anglo-Catholic tradition in the life of this church, such as a priest who was addressed as 'Father', and a rich diet of liturgical worship. I enjoyed being able to take communion twice a week in one place. And we celebrated the seasons of the church year with far more drama and excitement than I had ever previously experienced. But the informality of the building and its multiple roles in the community seemed to facilitate a blending of influences from different traditions. They used two hymn books: one which was Catho-lic in origin and one which was Evangelical. I very much appreciated this mixture. They were in need of a musician, and I soon took on the role of organist (for the traditional hymns) and pianist (for the contem-porary worship songs).

For the first time as a Christian, I found one church which seemed to address all the different aspects of my spirituality. There was joyful, lively singing. There were times of stillness and contemplation. There was thoughtful preaching and discussion. There was a strong emphasis on the sacrament of communion. There was beautiful liturgy. And there was a warm and encouraging community.

With that as my spiritual home, I made occasional visits to the evening services of other churches in central London. In particular, I sampled some of the more elaborate and ornate Anglo-Catholic worship that could be found. Solemn Evensong with Benediction at the famous Anglo-Catholic shrine of All Saints' Margaret Street was a favourite for a while. It was a stunningly decorated church, covered from floor to ceiling with pictures and mosaics, which would gradually fade from view behind the clouds of incense used in services. I began to notice that Catholic-style splendour, with beautiful liturgy and wonderful music, was actually much easier to find amongst Anglo-Catholics than among today's Roman Catholics. Occasional visits to Roman Catholic and Orthodox services were interesting experiences, but I did not find anything there which was absent from the Church of England.

Meanwhile, I occasionally visited some of the thriving Charismatic churches among the Church of England parishes of central London, enjoying the joyful exuberance of their worship and the optimism of their preaching. What I realised more and more was that the Church of England seemed to be able to hold together an amazingly wide set of traditions. I looked back on my years of exploring different kinds of churches, and realised that everything I had enjoyed and valued seemed to be represented somewhere within the Church of England.

And so I realised that I had found my spiritual home, and I chose to join. I was confirmed by the Bishop of London in a very moving ceremony. I said then, as I have often said since, that I joined the Church of England because of its breadth. The surprising thing to me, and one of the main reasons for writing this book, is that I have never met anyone else who says exactly that. Most other Anglicans identify themselves much more strongly with one particular faction within the Church. And in many cases they are very wary of the others, or almost entirely ignorant of them.

I moved next to teach in a village in Buckinghamshire, where I ended up being involved in several Church of England parishes. There was the team of rural churches where I lived, which had a dignified and traditional style of worship. And there was a lively Charismatic Evangelical church in a nearby town which I went to on Sunday evenings, where it was easier to find friends of my generation. I contributed to lots of church music of different kinds: sometimes playing the organ and directing a small choir, sometimes playing keyboard or flute for contemporary worship songs. It was a time when I began to feel calmly settled, and the uncertainties and the restlessness of the previous years began to fade into the background.

The time came when it seemed right to offer myself as a candidate for ordination in the Church of England and, after a long selection process, the Church of England agreed. But this reopened the old confusion about where exactly I belonged. I was happy being involved in contrasting churches, and was unable to label myself as being part of one particular group. Residential training for ordination in the Church of England is done by colleges which are firmly established within Evangelical and Anglo-Catholic factions, and I was told to pick one. It was a difficult decision for me, as I feared that three years of immersion in any one tradition would cause me to get annoyed with it.

In the end, I was delighted to discover an experimental new option, a part-time course spread over six years. This would run first alongside my teaching job and then alongside working three-quarter time in a church as a curate. The college in question, St John's in Nottingham, was Evangelical. And I was sent to a church in Oxford which was comfortably situated in the middle ground of the Church of England. I enjoyed the combination of the two experiences, and I felt at home in my church, which represented very well a generosity and breadth in its approach to Anglicanism.

In 2003, I moved to my current position as chaplain of Downing College, Cambridge. It was good to return to a university which had previously given me so much, and in which I could help others to explore faith as I had done. Once again, the Cambridge Inter-Collegiate Christian Union began to play a very significant role in my world, being the most well-attended focus for devout Christian students. Evangelical students are often suspicious of chaplains, and that has been a very challenging situation for me at times. But we mostly found that we could relate well to each other, and I found that I was also able to connect with Catholic students, with choir members, and with people from a diverse range of Christian and non-Christian backgrounds.

I run the Chapel as a place which is confidently rooted in the middle ground of the Church of England, and which from there is able to form helpful connections with a wide range of people. We have a routine of daily prayers, and Sunday services of Holy Communion and Choral Evensong. We have a choir and organ scholars who delight us with the splendours of the Anglican choral tradition. Until recently, we also had a music group of different instrumentalists which played in a more informal style at some services, but the current generation of students seems to find a traditional approach more interesting. Now we make a lot of use of the oldest English liturgies from the *Book of Common Prayer*.

I give talks and lead discussions about theology each week to students studying many different subjects and who have many different previous experiences of Christianity. The Chapel provides a meeting point for them to compare their perspectives and learn from each other. I help them to do that, and have refined over the years a way of explaining my middle-of-the-road Anglicanism. It provides a sign-post and a crossroads from which people can explore other parts of the Christian Church. It can be a polite way of mediating within various conflicts. But I also think that this central ground is of great significance in itself. And so my journey has at last led me to the writing of this book.

MAPPING THE TERRITORY: TWO QUESTIONS

That summary of my journey has highlighted some of the main features of the different approaches to the Christian faith taken by today's churches. As I found, it can be difficult to make sense of all this variety. Christianity has spread all around the world and has diversified into tens of thousands of denominations, many of which contain different perspectives within them.

Nevertheless, the most significant differences between today's churches can actually be traced back to only two big underlying questions. The answers to those questions given by each Christian group go a long way towards showing how that group compares with the others. The questions are:

1.   Were the doctrines and practices developed by the Roman Catholic Church from the first century until the 1950s the result of divine revelation or human invention?

2.   Has the liberalisation of society in recent centuries been inspired by God or is it rejection of divine authority?

In each case, the answer could involve confidently taking one of the two sides. My approach, of course, will be to say in each case that it is a bit of both, and that a book is needed in order to explore the strengths and weaknesses of each side of the argument. I have therefore structured this book around those two questions, with three chapters for each. But the rest of this chapter will introduce the significance of the ways in which different Christians answer those two questions.

The first question concerns the development of Catholicism. The opening 1500 years of Christian history saw the continuous story of the Roman Catholic Church, gradually developing its doctrines and ceremonies and consolidating its power over the whole of society, confident that this process was being led by the Holy Spirit. But, at the Reformation in the 16th century, Protestants claimed that the Church had in fact gone seriously astray, and sought to return to a simpler form of Christian faith found by reading the Bible. In response, the Catholic Church gave a robust reaffirmation of its approach, and continued over the following centuries to define new teachings which it considered to be the infallible work of the Holy Spirit. It did not start to turn in a more Protestant direction until the Second Vatican Council began in 1962.

Some examples of the teachings developed in that continuous process are:

•   The three-fold pattern of ordained Christian ministry in which churches are led by a male hierarchy of bishops, priests and deacons (established during the second century).

•   The choice of the 27 books and letters of the New Testament (second to fourth century).

•   The clear statement that Jesus Christ is both fully human and fully divine, rather than a human adopted by God, or an angelic being, or someone part-human and part-divine (formalised in the fourth century).

- The doctrine of the Trinity: God as the three equal persons of the Father, Son and Holy Spirit (fourth century).
- The development of liturgies: services with set prayers, readings and chants following daily, weekly and annual cycles, including the celebration of church seasons and saints' days (growing throughout the first millennium and the Middle Ages).
- An elaborate set of rituals for different occasions (including the list of seven sacraments finalised in the Middle Ages, such as marriage).
- The belief in transubstantiation: the change of the inward substance of bread and wine into the body and blood of Christ (defined in those terms in the thirteenth century).
- The authority of the Pope over all Christians (growing through the centuries leading up to the eleventh).
- The belief in the complete sinlessness of Mary since her conception (believed by many since the Middle Ages, made official in 1854), and her bodily assumption into heaven (proclaimed as an infallible doctrine in 1950).
- The dogma of the infallibility of the Pope (proclaimed in 1870).

This is a thought-provoking list, especially from a Protestant perspective. Fervent Protestants, when hearing my first question, may immediately want to answer that all Catholic traditions are human inventions, insisting that divine truth is only found in the Bible. But the formation of the Bible itself is an early part of that Catholic history, as are the formulations of the central doctrines about Jesus and the Trinity which are still accepted by Protestants as part of the correct way to interpret the New Testament. Medieval ceremonial practices have often been mocked by Protestants, but all churches continue the Catholic practice invented in the Middle Ages of holding weddings in churches, something never mentioned in the Bible.

So all Christians, including Protestants, accept some elements of Catholic tradition. They accept that the Holy Spirit has to some extent been at work in guiding the Catholic Church, especially in the formation of the New Testament, and so are to some extent picking and choosing from that list. All Christians are doing a bit more than just saying 'no' to it all: they are all somewhere along a scale from accepting a little of it to accepting all of it. Chapters Two to Four of this book will explore the various issues at stake in more detail.

The second question concerns the formation of modern society. In recent centuries, countries strongly influenced by Protestantism have led the way in valuing individual freedom much more highly. This transformation was energised by the Industrial Revolution, which greatly accelerated a series of social changes, including the development of democracy, the growth of equal rights and opportunities for women, and more recently the transformation of attitudes to homosexuality. And so the second question often cuts across the great denominational divides which opened up from the 16th century. It asks: Has the liberalisation of society in recent centuries been inspired by God or is it rejection of divine authority?

Again, by way of introduction, here are some examples of the main developments to which that question refers.

- The replacement of the absolute power of monarchs, aristocrats and established Churches by systems of democracy in which all men and women can vote.
- The ending of the death penalty and other sanctions against those who openly disagree with an established Christian Church.
- A belief in the importance of individual liberty, including the abolition of slavery.
- The admission of girls to secondary schools and then women to universities.
- The admission of women to traditionally male professions (e.g. doctors, lawyers, professors, politicians, leaders of churches).
- Widespread cohabitation and parenthood outside marriage.
- The availability of divorce with little or no social stigma.
- The ending of the death penalty for men having sex with men, and then the full legalisation of homosexuality.
- The social affirmation of same-sex relationships, including equal access to marriage.

- The acceptance of the use of modern contraceptive methods as an ordinary part of most people's lives.
- The normalisation of casual sex.
- Easy access to pornography, with a growing acceptance of its more extreme forms.
- A much greater contact with and respect for other cultures around the world, including their varied religious traditions.
- A tendency to ignore differences between faiths by regarding religious teachings as myth, poetry and moral fables, rather than taking their truth claims literally.
- The secularisation of society, in which questions about the meaning of life are understood to be private matters which do not belong in the public sphere, and in which any attempts to bring religion back into shared spaces and conversations appear rude or threatening.
- The condemnation of Christian missionary work as a form of Western imperialism.
- The belief that whatever form of eternal salvation exists will inevitably be received by all people (universalism).

Again this list may contain a few surprises. Enthusiasts for progress may still find one or two things to feel uneasy about. And those who like to think of themselves as traditionalists may nevertheless be very protective of their individual rights and freedoms and the education of their daughters.

The world has changed greatly since the Bible was written, and its authors would not have felt instantly at home with any of the developments I have listed. But it would be extremely hard to find any Christian today who did not see at least one of those changes as a positive and godly step. So we are all to some extent recognising divine goodness at work in the developments of society, and are somewhere on a scale from accepting a little of that list to accepting most or even all of it.

THE TWO QUESTIONS AND THE TEACHINGS OF JESUS

Both questions are important ones which all Christians are somehow answering whether or not they realise it. And these are not just some random quirks of history and human debate: they relate to important ideas that are there at the beginning in the teachings of Jesus.

The first question connects with our interpretation of Jesus' words when he said this to the disciples: 'When the Spirit of truth comes, he will guide you into all the truth.'[3] Jesus promised that the Spirit would continue his work of guiding his followers, but the Gospels do not describe the details of how that would happen. The most cautious Protestant interpretation says that the Spirit went on to inspire the writing of the New Testament, after which his only work has been to help people to understand it. The more expansive Roman Catholic view is that the Spirit has not only inspired the Scriptures and guided the Church in their correct interpretation, but has also revealed further truths over the centuries. But Jesus did not explicitly say either of those things, mentioning neither the writing and compilation of a New Testament, nor the formation of an infallible Papacy. In addressing my first question, all Christian theology involves some kind of a judgement about the way in which the Spirit has guided the Church.

The second question connects with our interpretation of Jesus' words when he proclaimed the arrival of the Kingdom of God on earth. He said that it would develop like a mustard seed growing into a huge tree, and like yeast making bread rise.[4] He described a transformation of the world associated with his concern for social justice,[5] the inclusion of outsiders,[6] and an overturning of hierarchies in which the last would become first[7] and the meek would inherit the earth.[8] Alongside that, he also spoke of the world in his time as being ruled by evil.[9] It is reasonable, therefore, to expect Christianity to have some positive

3   John 16.13
4   Matthew 13.31-33
5   e.g. Luke 4.18
6   e.g. Luke 5.27-32
7   e.g. Luke 13.30
8   Matthew 5.5
9   e.g. John 17.14-15

impact on society, and to see the Spirit at work to bring reconciliation, inclusion, social justice and an end to oppression, as well as to find forces in the world which are hostile to God's work. In addressing my second question, all Christian theology involves some kind of a judgement about the ways in which the Spirit has been at work in changing the world around us.

So I think that these are important questions, and that people of intelligence, integrity and good faith have come up with a range of interesting answers to both of them. Looking at how people answer those two questions opens up a useful way of mapping the landscape of Christian faith today.

A CHART WITH TWO AXES FOR TWO QUESTIONS

When people start noticing the differences between churches, the first judgement they usually make concerns whether a church seems modern or traditional. This tends to be the most obvious thing about any particular place of worship, and about the image which its congregation is seeking to present to visitors. So a brick-built church with cheerful carpets, upholstered chairs, large clear windows and a stage with a drum kit and a vast video projection screen seems very different from a Gothic stone building with carved pews, an ornate altar, Latin inscriptions and stained-glass images of medieval saints. The first may seem adventurous and progressive, while the second may give a sense that nothing has changed for many centuries.

The truth is often far more complicated than that, however. In reality, the modern-looking church may be the one which refuses to let women preach. And the ancient-looking church may be the one led by a female priest who enjoys blessing same-sex marriages. This sort of thing often confuses people for a very long time. In my experience, it takes a lot of determination to make any sense of it.

To begin to get our bearings within the landscape of today's churches, a single scale from traditional to modern can be very misleading. It is a lot more helpful to think of two different scales, forming two axes of a chart, following the answers to the two questions I have been describing.

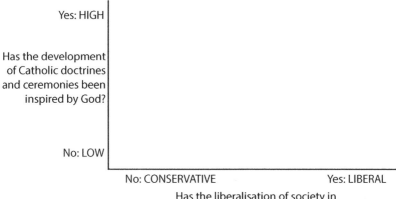

On the vertical axis, we have the Protestant and Catholic views about revelation to the Church over the centuries, and the labels fit usefully with the way that those perspectives are often also called *low church* and *high church*. On the horizontal axis, we have the judgement about the Spirit's work in transforming human society, which I have labelled as *conservative* and *liberal*. Please note that those terms in this context have nothing at all to do with political slogans and political party names (which have a complicated history and have sometimes travelled a long way from their original meanings). In this context, I am using conservative to mean being cautious about change and wanting to preserve a unified society built of tried and tested traditions. And I am using liberal to mean valuing the freedom of individuals and being very confident about the progress which will result from that freedom.

Putting them together opens up a big space within which various viewpoints can be identified. The ones at the four corners are often described in this way:

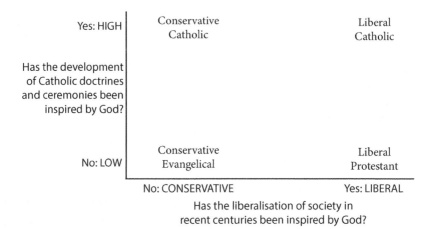

So we can now look at each of those four perspectives individually.

CONSERVATIVE CATHOLICISM

In a way, this is the clearest and most obvious position to take, being very confident about God's work within his Church. It has a seamless history going right back to the early Church without any interruption, and is the official position of the denomination containing the majority of the world's Christians. It therefore has a strong claim to be the default option. Catholicism and conservatism fit smoothly together, since Catholics have a very confident view of the teachings established by the Church in past centuries. From this perspective, the formation of the New Testament, the development of beliefs about Mary, the formation of elaborate liturgies and the proclamation of the infallibility of the Pope are all part of the same unbroken process of revelation.

This confidence in Christian tradition puts conservative Catholics at odds with some developments in modern society which are embraced by more liberal churches. Christians were for many centuries unanimous that women could never become priests, and conservative Catholics see that as cast-iron evidence that this view was revealed by

God as his will for all time. So the Roman Catholic hierarchy today sees the ordination of woman as a subject which is not even open to debate. Similarly, there is a deeply established condemnation of all forms of sexual activity outside heterosexual marriage or involving contraception.

The Roman Catholic Church has moved in a more liberal direction in recent times, as I will describe in the next section, and individual Catholics are very often far more liberal than the official teachings of their Church. But conservative Catholics still exist in large numbers. Many were encouraged by the revived support for the traditional Latin Mass given by Pope Benedict XVI in 2007, the central part of a resurgence of interest in more traditional and distinctive forms of Catholicism.

LIBERAL CATHOLICISM

Since Catholicism is officially so confident about its teachings established in the past, liberal Catholicism may sound like an impossibility. Yet liberal views are widely found among individual Roman Catholics, especially in Western countries. And Pope Francis is famous for strongly hinting at possible reforms, such as saying 'Who am I to judge?' when asked about homosexuality. The Second Vatican Council (1962-5) led to simper forms of service in modern languages and better relationships with Protestants and other faiths, affirming religious freedom and abandoning the old assumption that there is no salvation outside the Roman Catholic Church. It produced some revolutionary changes which many Catholics are hoping will one day go much further.

My next point involves stretching the definitions of church labels almost to breaking point, but I must note that a liberal Catholic approach has a significant presence among Protestants, especially Anglicans. I apologise if you need to reread that sentence several times. Although Protestants do not accept the authority of the Pope, there are some who have a high-church enthusiasm for many of the traditional ceremonies of the Catholic Church, as I found in my explorations of churches. Anglo-Catholics often have an ornate style of worship which contains many of the features which the Roman Catholics began to get rid of in the 1960s. Some of them now look much more Catholic than today's

Pope. They are sometimes also interested in the ancient and medieval philosophy which fed into the history of Catholic theology. Yet, as members of churches which are Protestant (even though they may carefully avoid using that term), they are much freer to lean in a liberal direction on modern social issues. These are the people whom you may find blessing gay marriages using incense and Latin plainchant, or who have Masses celebrated by women priests. Liberal Catholicism can also be a very artistic and aesthetic approach to Christianity, valuing the beauties of traditional Christian worship while seeing it as inherently symbolic, pointing to divine truths which are beyond words.

In a sense, this is the most optimistic form of Christianity, believing both that God has been powerfully at work through the development of the Church, and that God is powerfully at work in many aspects of the development of modern society.

CONSERVATIVE EVANGELICALISM

In the opposite corner, taking a cautious view of both questions, conservative Evangelicals have a much more minimalist approach. Theirs is in many ways the most straightforward way of being Christian, arguably in keeping with the simple and direct methods of Jesus in his travelling ministry as a teacher. They dismiss the rich and complex traditions of Catholic history, and are nervous about our society's habit of reinventing itself in ways which keep getting further from the Bible's frame of reference. They aim to keep their focus on the message about salvation from sin which they find in the Scriptures. They do so by proclaiming the crucifixion of Jesus Christ, with a theology built around the doctrine of justification by faith. The term Evangelical relates to their commitment to communicating the Christian message to the whole world.

Conservative Evangelicals often have a very pragmatic, inventive and unsentimental view of things like church buildings and forms of worship, adopting whatever methods seem to work best in getting the message across in their local context. If guitars, drums, big screens and comfy chairs can help to gather a crowd today to learn about Jesus, then guitars, drums, big screens and comfy chairs are the way to go for the time being. In such a bright and modern context, some of the crowd will then be quite surprised when they eventually notice that there are never any women on the platform in positions of leadership.

Conservative Evangelicals are confident that they are simply believing what the Bible says. But I will argue in this book that they are still partly dependent on early elements of Catholic tradition, and heavily dependent on a set of Protestant theological traditions developed from the 16th century. They also tend not to notice the ways in which they have already assimilated some of the earlier social changes brought about by liberalism.

LIBERAL PROTESTANTISM

Without a pope to shepherd the whole movement, Protestantism has always tended to diversify and divide. Many Evangelicals are in varying degrees more liberal than those in the conservative corner I described above, and a wide spectrum of different approaches can be found among Protestants as a whole.

Of all the four corners, this one has the weakest sense of identity. It is not marked out from the rest of the world by elaborate medieval ceremonial traditions, or by a way of loudly and confidently summing up the Gospel, or by a stubborn resistance to social change. Liberal Protestants often focus on matters of social justice and environmental responsibility in the present rather than on a spiritual message about admission to a heavenly afterlife. They tend to cooperate very happily with non-Christian organisations and community groups seeking human wellbeing, meaning that their understanding of the Gospel blurs easily into a general support for charities, for the state, or for campaigns for human rights and green issues.

If liberal Protestants think about life after death, they are quite likely to be universalists, believing or hoping that all will somehow go to heaven in the end. Their worship is often informal, with no great importance attached to any particular traditions or holy places. But they enjoy the greatest freedom of all four groups, and can draw freely from the resources of the other three in any way they choose.

NEIGHBOURS AND OPPOSITES

Members of any two groups which are neighbours on the chart should easily find some things that they have in common, such as a shared support for women's ministry on the right of the diagram, or a love of liturgy at the top of the diagram, or a trust in historic revelation at the left, or a preference for informal worship along the bottom.

The most difficult relationships occur between those who are diagonally opposite. Conservative Catholics and liberal Protestants have a very simple and direct contrast with each other, which is at least easy to understand. The conservative Catholics are likely to see the opposite corner as a faith that has been watered down and secularised almost beyond recognition. And the liberal Protestants are likely to look back in amazement at those who seem to them like reactionary and irrational fanatics who have suddenly appeared in a time machine from the Middle Ages.

But the greatest level of bewilderment and misunderstanding occurs between the liberal Catholics and the conservative Evangelicals who form the other pair of diagonal opposites. Each group is selectively very definite about some things and very relaxed about some other things, but the selections do not greatly overlap. The conservative Evangelicals are very definite about the importance of sound doctrine in establishing a lively faith in Jesus that brings salvation, while not caring much about the details of ceremonies and rituals. Meanwhile, the liberal Catholics tend to approach doctrine through the mysteries and ambiguities of poetry and symbolism, cheerfully assuming that most or all people will probably go to heaven, at the same time as having enthusiastically precise tastes in liturgies, robes and ceremonial traditions, often combined with strong views on social justice. The conservative Evangelicals may suspect that the other corner is just enjoying dressing up and has never really encountered Jesus. And the liberal Catholics may suspect that the other corner just enjoys shouting simplistic slogans and cannot fathom the depths of an authentic spirituality. Interestingly, both groups are trying to talk about the human relationship with God as something that is both reliably universal and deeply personal, but their contrasting deployments of certainty and vagueness mean that they usually find it very hard to work together.

SOME FURTHER COMPLEXITIES

I have sketched out the four corners, but of course those are the extremes. Many Christians are further towards the middle in some form, and I will be exploring that territory throughout the book. Evangelicalism, for example, often extends out beyond its conservative corner in the direction of liberalism, sometimes being known as 'open Evangelicalism'. Many Evangelical churches have women ministers, and many preach about social justice and environmental issues as well as the eternal salvation of the individual.

If I had holographic printing and another dimension to play with, the best candidate for a third axis would be the emphasis on the miraculous work of the Holy Spirit placed by Pentecostals and Charismatics. Although this theme has been widely influential across other churches, it is primarily located as an option within Evangelicalism, so that is how I will discuss it in this book.

Orthodox Christians may have the best grounds for being annoyed that I have not given them a special mention so far, since they trace their own unbroken tradition back to the early Church. But it remains the case that, from a Protestant perspective, Orthodoxy mostly looks like Catholicism without the Pope and with an even more elaborate set of ceremonial traditions. So I will only have space here to describe it primarily in relation to the history of Catholicism.

Finally, when using the labels *conservative* and *liberal*, it is worth emphasising again that those really do not map tidily onto any current political movements (including the Conservative Party and the Liberal Democrats in the UK as they are today). There are indeed some tribal allegiances between different Christian groups and different political parties in various countries. But those allegiances owe much more to the quirks of local histories than to any underlying universal truths. For example, Evangelicals in America are usually right-wing, but are much more likely to be left-wing in the UK.

Having noted these complexities, I now arrive at my main theme: the middle ground.

THE CENTRE AND THE CHURCH OF ENGLAND

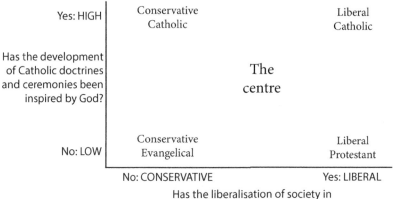

This book explores a perspective which seems to me to be in the middle of the four approaches, drawing on their strengths and rejecting their weaknesses. It is a perspective that can be enjoyed from the middle ground of the Church of England. As I have described, I like the fact that the Church of England is spread most of the way across the diagram. Other Protestant denominations have tended to split apart repeatedly in the search for doctrinal purity and have become narrower. For various reasons which have changed over the centuries, the Church of England has often worked unusually hard to hold people together from different perspectives.

Originally that owed much to Queen Elizabeth I (reign: 1558-1603) wanting to unite her people. Then perhaps there was also an English knack for living together on a very crowded little island while trying not to get in each other's way too much. I think it also has something to do with an English seafaring love of exploring the world and shamelessly copying impressive parts of other people's cultures. Our most zealous reformers may have smashed up our Catholic art in the 16th century, but by the 18th century it was normal for wealthy young men to go on Grand Tours of Europe, looking admiringly at Italian altarpieces and Renaissance frescos, all of which enlarged their perspectives and helped to prepare the way for the great Anglo-Catholic revival of the 19th century.

So the Church of England offers me a very helpful setting from which to look out across the varied landscape of Christian faith. But I am not going to attempt to define the True Essence of Anglicanism as it is practiced around the world in the various sister Churches which comprise the Anglican Communion. I am not going to analyse the various agreed statements of international Anglican committees from the last century or so. Nor am I going to wade into any debates about the correct interpretation of the great 16th-century English theologians. There are enough books that do those sorts of thing, and even I tend to find that they often get a bit dull.

The fact is that a great many Anglicans are out towards the various edges of my diagram. And many of them do not value the diversity which I find so interesting, preferring to think that their particular corner is the only one that should be there. Around the world, different parts of the Anglican Communion are often strongly linked to only one tradition, derived from the tradition of whichever missionary society brought the faith to that place. Many will therefore see my approach as rather eccentric. Most American Anglicans in their Episcopal Church will probably think that I use the dreaded word 'Protestant' far too enthusiastically, while their Nigerian counterparts are more likely to see me as a dangerous liberal.

Meanwhile, much of what I am arguing for could happily be adopted by a high-church Methodist or an ecumenically-minded Lutheran, and it is not far removed from the beliefs of many ordinary Catholics who use contraception and never go to confession. So this is my view from territory that seems to me to be somewhere in the middle of Christianity as a whole.

Nevertheless, part of my aim is to correct a widely-held set of misconceptions about the middle ground of the Church of England, which has become my beloved home. There is an unhelpful habit among Anglicans of using a one-dimensional scale to classify churches, simply going from high to low. This clearly positions the conservative

Evangelicals at one end of the line and the conservative Anglo-Catholics at the other, and assumes that there is a sort of vague liberal mushiness in the middle. This oversimplification causes both sets of conservatives to be surprised on the rare occasions when they bump into each other and rediscover how much they have in common. And it leads to enormous confusion over what on earth is going on in the mixed-up middle, where too many different issues have been blurred together and there is a desperate lack of clarity.

There is an urgent need for the middle ground to be mapped and defined more clearly. Opening up my two-dimensional diagram, my task will be to make an appreciative but critical assessment of Catholics, Evangelicals, conservatives and liberals, and to define a clear and coherent theological position among them.

THE SHAPE OF THE BOOK

The rest of this book explores those vertical and horizonal axes in more detail, with three chapters for each. Chapters Two to Four look at the axis from low church to high church, discussing the different perspectives developed by Protestants and Catholics. In Chapter Two, I describe the Church as a community which is both global and local, bringing together the Catholic tendency to think first of a worldwide hierarchy and the Protestant tendency to think first of the faith of the individual and the local group. Chapter Three takes me to the heart of the Reformation argument about salvation by faith or by works, looking at divine action and human response, and at the role of sacraments. And Chapter Four explores the ways in which Christian spirituality is thought to be shaped either by traditions revealed over centuries or by a lively and informal encounter with the Holy Spirit in the present moment.

Then, for the remaining three chapters, I look at the differences of perspective on social changes that have opened up in recent centuries, along my horizontal axis between conservatives and liberals. Chapter Five focuses on the transformation of the lives of women and compares the conservative allegiance to traditional ways of life with the liberal campaign for equality. Chapter Six looks at our understanding of human sexuality as it loses its traditional anchor in the procreation of children. And Chapter Seven looks at the Church's task of proclaiming the Gospel to the whole world: is this now to be replaced by a liberal love of pluralism and a belief in universal salvation?

If you are especially interested in the issues which people argue most about today, you may wish to jump ahead to Chapter Four. Human nature being what it is, you may have already browsed through Chapter Six's thoughts on sex. But Chapters Two and Three lay some important foundations in describing how the earliest divisions among Christians took shape, and these will help to make more sense of the later chapters.

All six questions will open up ancient and modern insights into the Bible and how we should interpret it. As I tackle each of those questions, I will discuss the strengths and weaknesses of both sides, and gradually build up a picture of a middle way which can draw out the best of all of them.

SUGGESTIONS FOR FURTHER READING

Conservative Catholicism

Conservatives have a very confident sense that religion is a body of revealed truth which can be presented systematically. The definitive, detailed account of the official teachings of the Roman Catholic Church is the *Catechism of the Catholic Church*, first approved by Pope John Paul II in 1992. The most recent English edition was published by Libreria Editrice Vaticana in 2019. Though weighty, it has a very clear structure, a direct and straightforward style, and an excellent index, making it an easy book to explore.

The various writings of Pope John Paul II (reigned 1978-2005) and his successor Pope Benedict XVI (reigned 2005-2013) also give an authoritative glimpse of conservative Catholicism. For a strong example of the boldness, rigour and insight of this tradition, try *Love and Responsibility* by John Paul II, writing before his papacy with the name Karol Wojtyla (reprinted 1993, Ignatius Press). Wojtyla argues for a traditional Catholic understanding of family life and sexual morality, presenting the human person as deserving of love and not objectification.

Liberal Catholicism

A very clear overview of the whole Christian faith from a liberal Anglo-Catholic perspective can be found in *This is our Faith: A Popular Presentation of Anglican Belief* written by Rosemary Gallagher, Jeffrey John and John Trenchard (2014, Redemptorist Publications). It describes the seven Catholic sacraments in detail, while affirming same-sex relationships and the ordination of women.

Other liberal Anglo-Catholics may share similar beliefs but are much more wary of anything systematic. Mark Oakley's approach to theology through poetry and literature is a good example, found in *The Collage of God* (2012, Canterbury Press) and *The Splash of Words: Believing in Poetry* (2016, Canterbury Press). Oakley sees faith as a collage in which the picture is built up from lots of fragments of ideas and experiences, rather than from a clearly revealed framework.

In the Roman Catholic Church, liberal theology is a somewhat sensitive area. Hans Küng, an adviser at the Second Vatican Council, was famously banned from continuing to teach as a Catholic theologian in 1978 after he wrote a book arguing against papal infallibility. A liberal approach to Roman Catholicism is easiest to find in writings about popular spirituality, such as the works of Gerard W. Hughes, including his excellent *God of Surprises* (2008, Darton, Longman and Todd) or Richard Rohr, such as *The Universal Christ* (2019, SPCK).

Conservative Evangelicalism

For a powerful counterweight to the *Catechism of the Catholic Church*, I recommend Wayne Grudem's *Systematic Theology: An Introduction to Biblical Doctrine* (2020, IVP). Similarly, it is an impressively heavy volume which is well organised and easy to dip into for answers to specific questions. Among more moderate size volumes, Timothy Keller's *The Reason for God* (2009, Hodder and Stoughton) gives a robust and intelligent account of Christianity from a conservative Protestant perspective.

The most significant figure in recent conservative Evangelicalism in the Church of England was John Stott (1921-2011). I think he may have had more impact on the Church of England than anyone else in his lifetime. He is known especially for *The Cross of Christ* (2006, IVP), a very detailed study of biblical teaching on the atonement. His much smaller book on *Basic Christianity* (2013, IVP) has been especially popular.

Moving a step in a liberal direction (including affirming women as leaders of churches), is Tom Wright, whose writings set the New Testament very helpfully in its historical context and show its relevance for today. Good examples of his many books are *Simply Christian* (2006, SPCK) and *Scripture and the Authority of God* (2013, SPCK).

Liberal Protestantism

Liberal Protestantism is diverse, open and hard to define, but social justice and environmentalism are often the most definite themes today. Books produced by the Iona Community provide many examples, such as the *Wild Goose Big Book of Worship Resources* (2017, Wild Goose Publications).

Liberal Protestantism has always valued individual experiences of faith and spirituality, and a robust defence of that approach against atheist critics can be found in *Unapologetic: Why, despite everything, Christianity can still make surprising emotional sense* by Francis Spufford (2012, Faber and Faber).

Popular current American writers include Rob Bell, author of *Love Wins* (2011, Collins), who has become controversial among Evangelicals for expressing increasingly liberal views. Meanwhile, Nadia Bolz-Weber, author of *Accidental Saints: Finding God in All the Wrong People* (2015, Canterbury Press), combines liturgical Lutheranism with a gift for connecting with those alienated by conservative faith.

I should also mention an earlier form of liberal Protestantism which reached the peak of its influence in the Church of England in the 1970s. It was very dogmatic in its rejection of traditional Christian beliefs (such as the virgin birth and resurrection of Jesus), calling for a 'non-realist' understanding of God, or the demythologising of the Bible, or the reinterpretation of Christianity in terms of existentialism. Widely read books included John Robinson's *Honest to God* (1963, SCM), *The Myth of God Incarnate* edited by John Hick (1977, SCM), and Don Cupitt's *Sea of Faith* (1984, BBC Books). But this form of liberalism has mostly failed to inspire churchgoers in any lasting way, so it does not feature in the debates which shape this book.

The Centre

I have written this book because there is a lack of authors who confidently adopt a central perspective. The most famous writer who described himself in those terms is C. S. Lewis (1898-1963), known for the Christian themes of his *Chronicles of Narnia*, as well as for his popular Christian books. He said:

> I am a very ordinary layman of the Church of England, not especially 'high', nor especially 'low', nor especially anything else.

This comes from the preface to his *Mere Christianity* (2012, Collins), where he seeks to introduce the main teachings which all Christians have in common.

Anglicanism

For more details about Anglicanism, its history and the way it works today as a global communion, Mark Chapman is a good guide. Try *Anglicanism: A Very Short Introduction* (2006, Oxford) first, then for more details see *Anglican Theology* (2012, T&T Clark).

What Anglicans Believe: An Introduction by Samuel Wells (2011, Canterbury Press) is concise, balanced and insightful.

For a much more wide-ranging exploration, see *The Oxford Handbook of Anglican Studies* edited by Mark Chapman, Sathianathan Clarke and Martyn Percy (2015, Oxford University Press), with contributions from many different writers.

For a fascinating variety of personal experiences, see the individual contributions to *Why I am Still an Anglican*, edited by Caroline Chartres (2011, Continuum).

Chapter Two
The Church: Global and Local

It is possible to think about the Christian Church from two opposite perspectives. The first perspective sees it primarily as a single worldwide institution, a clearly identified global organisation. This organisation is united across time as well as space: it has a history which shows a continuous succession of leaders going back to Jesus and the apostles. This perspective then goes on to see that the one vast and historic structure of the Church contains many local parishes and many individual faithful Christians in particular places in the present.

The second perspective starts at the smallest level in the here and now. It thinks first of the individual people who have faith in Jesus today, and of the local church fellowships in which those believers choose to meet together. Only after that does it go on to consider ways which those believers and congregations may then join forces on a regional, national or international scale. It looks carefully at the Bible, but most of the time shows very little awareness of the history of the Church between the New Testament and the present.

The first is the Catholic view, a top-down view which sees God working in a universal way through one visible institution, and through its teachings and history. The second is a bottom-up view which has been gradually enabled by Protestantism, believing that all Christians should read the Bible for themselves. It emphasises the work of the Holy Spirit in the lives of individuals, thinking of the global Church as something whose true membership is known only to God.

The top-down view, which I will call 'high church', attributes great importance to the details of the traditions that have evolved through the Church's visible history. It offers a splendid hierarchy of popes, cardinals, archbishops, bishops, priests and laypeople, and a shared set of elaborate ceremonial customs. Being a Catholic is about being part of that global community: being in communion with the Pope, and following the established authority of the Catholic Church, using the same prayers and readings in the Mass that Catholics throughout the world use. And so a local church is only understood to be a local church because it participates in the life of that global institution and the ministry of its bishops.

The bottom-up view, which I will call 'low church', sees ecclesiastical structures and ceremonial trappings as things which are usually dull, rarely relevant, and sometimes quite corrupt and sinister. Among the lowest-church Protestants, local churches may function completely independently. But most have a habit of joining forces with others within some kind of denomination or other big grouping, perhaps at least for an annual summer camp or conference, or for the training of ministers. But a low-church approach thinks that these bigger groupings only mean anything because of the local churches that join in, and because of the faith of the individuals within them.

In fact, the organisation of churches is probably the single biggest set of disagreements among different kinds of Christian. All this diversity has arisen because Jesus himself is recorded as saying very little on the subject. He tended to say things like, 'Whoever wants to be first must be last of all and servant of all,'[10] and never went into details like 'No person shall be capable of receiving the appointment of archdeacon until he has been six years complete in holy orders.'[11]

As the Catholic Church grew in its early centuries, it did evolve a detailed system. But when Protestants began to query the Catholic approach and thought that they could go back to the Bible for something more authentic, they found that the New Testament contained only a few clues, and they began to interpret those clues in lots of different ways.

The history of these different approaches is a useful way in to understanding the high and low perspectives, revealing a lot about the differences between Catholics and the various kinds of Protestant.

10   Mark 9.35
11   Canon C22 of the Church of England

THE NEW TESTAMENT

One thing that all Christians agree about is the list of 27 books which form the New Testament. We know that Christians were beginning to use these texts in their worship and their theology in the second century. They accepted them as being genuine statements of the teachings of Jesus and the apostles.

In particular, the four Gospels and the main letters of Paul were accepted as authoritative early on. But the status of books like Hebrews, James, the Second and Third Letters of John and the Book of Revelation was uncertain for a lot longer. There were a few other texts which floated in and out of favour in different places at different times, such as the *Shepherd of Hermas*. But during the fourth and fifth centuries, a consensus developed across the whole Church about the final definitive list, which we now call the canon of the New Testament. These books are the foundational documents of the Church. They are the best historical records relating to Jesus, and they are the texts which most clearly expressed the faith of the early Church and the message it had received from him, since Jesus himself did not write a book. These are the books which bear witness most authentically to Jesus Christ, his teachings and his impact on the world in a way which no others ever could. And so for all Christians, together with the Old Testament books which set the scene for Jesus' work and teaching, these are the texts which can be used in worship and in the development of doctrine, in a way which sets them apart from all others.

However, while the Church was developing the New Testament, it was also working out various other things. And the early Christians thought that God was guiding all of these processes. Conservative Evangelicals often make it sound as if the Bible fell out of the sky in its finished form soon after the Day of Pentecost, nicely printed in a single volume, so that people then began to follow its instructions. But the early Church's way of reading the Bible was developing at the same time as the early Church's decisions about the texts which belonged in the Bible. The Bible and a traditional approach to understanding the Bible were both taking shape at the same time.

CHURCH GOVERNMENT IN THE EARLY CHURCH

If we look at what the New Testament says about how to run churches, we do not find any kind of constitution, or rule book or code of canon law. What we find is that various things seem to have been happening in a rather unsystematic, ad hoc sort of way in the first century. The Church was growing rapidly, but often having to hide from persecution. And things to do with roles and structures seem to have been worked out in different ways in different places as people went on. Various titles are used, but without any detailed definitions. So Paul writes about apostles, prophets, evangelists, pastors and teachers[12] without saying much about how those roles should work. They seem to be very practical roles, based on the gifts that people had and on the needs that churches encountered.

Elsewhere, there are titles which seem to suggest an ordered structure of people in authority. There are *elders* and *overseers*, who are in positions of leadership. And they are meant to be treated with respect and need to be of good character.[13] And there are *deacons*,[14] whose title means assistants or helpers. The Greek word for elder, *presbuteros*, simply means someone who is older, but it has shaped the English words *priest* and *presbyter*, which are used in different ways today by different Christian traditions. And from the Greek word for overseer, *episkopos*, we get the English word *bishop* and the related term *episcopal*.

Most Christian churches make use of at least some of those words derived from the New Testament: priest, presbyter, bishop, deacon, apostle, prophet, evangelist, pastor, minister and so on. But none of those words has a definitive biblical job description behind it, so Protestant churches have revived these titles in a bewildering variety of ways. One church's elders might have the same role as another church's deacons, and arguments may break out about whether someone calling himself an apostle today could be following the guidance of the Holy Spirit or just making things up.

---

12   Ephesians 4.11
13   1 Timothy 3.2, 5.17
14   Acts 6.1-6, 1 Timothy 3.8-10

Although the first-century Church described in the New Testament seemed to lack any kind of clear constitution, things do appear to have settled down during the second century. The pattern that emerged was a hierarchical one, based on the leadership of bishops. While the New Testament seems to use the title of overseer/bishop in the same sort of way as elder/presbyter/priest, the two separated into different orders of ministry in the second century. So there would be one overseer/bishop for a city or area, in charge of a council of elders/presbyters/priests, who were all assisted by the deacons. This is the threefold pattern of the ministry of bishops, priests and deacons which is much-loved by high-church people today, and remains a distinctive feature of the Catholic, Orthodox and Anglican churches.

We can learn more about the developing role of bishops from letters written in the early Church, the first generation after the apostolic letters which were incorporated into the New Testament. For example, St Ignatius of Antioch became bishop of Antioch in about 69 AD, and he wrote a series of letters on the way to his martyrdom in 108 AD. Like St Paul, Ignatius wrote to the Romans and to the Ephesians. He also wrote a Letter to the Magnesians, in which he says:

> Let me urge on you the need for godly unanimity in everything you do. Let the bishop preside in the place of God, and his clergy in the place of the Apostolic conclave, and let my special friends the deacons be entrusted with the service of Jesus Christ.... Maintain absolute unity with your bishop and leaders.[15]

And in his Letter to the Smyrnaeans, he wrote:

> You must all follow the bishop as Jesus Christ followed the Father... Only that Eucharist which is under the authority of the bishop (or whomever he himself designates) is to be considered valid. Wherever the bishop appears, there let the congregation be; just as wherever Jesus Christ is, there is the catholic church.[16]

15   Letter of St Ignatius to the Magnesians, chapter 6 – this translation from Maxwell Staniforth (1968) *Early Christian Writings* Penguin Books

16   Letter of St Ignatius to the Smyrnaeans, chapter 8 – this translation from Michael W Holmes (2007) *The Apostolic Fathers* Baker Academic

So here in 108 AD is an early use of the word *catholic*, which is Greek for 'according to the whole', meaning universal. Ignatius sees the bishops as having a particular concern for the unity of the whole Church. To be part of this universal Church, the catholic Church, meant being united under the leadership of the local bishop. And the central act of Christian worship, the Eucharist (in other words, the Communion or the Mass), was to be presided over by the bishop or by someone to whom he had delegated the task.

This early emphasis on the divine authority of bishops may surprise many Protestants. But it is not an implausible development from the approach taken shortly beforehand in the New Testament letters. The apostle Paul wrote: 'Be imitators of me, as I am of Christ.'[17] And the First Letter of Peter tells people to accept the authority of the elders.[18]

It was natural for the early Church to consider its leaders to be the successors of the apostles, handing on the teachings received from Jesus' first disciples and inheriting their authority. And it was obvious to them that there was a clear, visible line of succession going back to the founder. Jesus had appointed apostles, who had themselves established churches and had appointed leaders. So each generation of leaders ordained further leaders to continue the tradition. This pattern is what has become known as the apostolic succession. High-church people like the idea that today's bishops are part of an unbroken chain which stretches back to Jesus Christ and the apostles. Catholic, Orthodox and Anglican bishops can say that they have been consecrated by earlier bishops laying hands on them and praying, who had themselves been consecrated by earlier bishops laying hands on them and praying, who were linked through that same process repeated over many generations all the way back to those who were consecrated by the apostles laying hands on them and praying. Low-church people prefer to say that the apostolic succession is all about being faithful to the apostles' teachings found in the New Testament, regardless of who has touched who on the head.

17   1 Corinthians 11.1
18   1 Peter 5.5

This three-fold structure of bishops, priests and deacons seems to have settled in all around the Church by the middle of the second century. It is not defined in the Bible, but it took shape before the New Testament took shape. Most Protestants ignore it, because it does not appear in the Scriptures. They trust that the early Christians were faithfully following the directions of the Holy Spirit when they compiled those Scriptures, but assume that the early Christians had been making things up using their own human inventiveness or cravings for power when they developed episcopal church government.

During the persecutions it faced in the early centuries, the Church also faced the difficult question of what to do if its leaders renounced their faith when threatened by the authorities. The Romans would from time to time arrest Christians and offer them an opportunity to curse Christ and to worship the emperor, executing those who stubbornly refused. Those who went to their deaths proclaiming their faith provided a great demonstration of the authenticity and power of their beliefs, and were venerated as martyrs by the early Christians. But that left the awkward question of what to do with the people who denied their faith in order to save their earthly lives. What should happen if they subsequently asked to resume their old places in the Church?

There were some who took a very unforgiving approach to this question. They demanded especially high standards of Christian leaders, and said that the prayers of those who had renounced their faith would now be ineffective. Such a priest would no longer be able to administer a valid baptism or preside over a genuine eucharist. If a bishop who had once renounced his faith then tried to resume his ministry, he would not be a real bishop, and priests subsequently ordained by him would not be real priests.

But a more forgiving approach prevailed. St Augustine (354 to 430 AD) was among those who argued that these ceremonial actions depended entirely on the grace of God, not the spiritual state of the minister. Someone who had been baptised by a heretic would still have received a real baptism, and would not need to have that baptism repeated. And the ordination of deacons, priests and bishops brought about a permanent change which could not be undone by any failings of those individuals, however serious.

I will return to this view of sacraments bringing permanent changes in the next chapter. For now, it is important to know that the Church in its early centuries formed the view that Christian ministry follows a hierarchical pattern established by God, in which God guarantees that his grace will flow through the actions of those who are correctly ordained by bishops. It arose as a generous and confident understanding of the scope of God's work through the Church, and was a great reassurance to those who were risking their lives for their allegiance to Jesus Christ.

FROM PERSECUTION TO ESTABLISHMENT: COUNCILS OF BISHOPS

Circumstances changed greatly in the fourth century, when the Roman Empire stopped persecuting the Church and went on to adopt Christianity as its established religion. A great alliance between Christianity and worldly power began to develop. People have a range of strong opinions about whether or not that was a good thing, and low-church people often see it as a very dubious partnership which corrupted the Church. Christianity now took on the new role of providing the shared belief system for the Roman Empire, and therefore the smooth running of the Church became a key factor in the smooth running of the Empire. This new alliance had enormous significance for most of the subsequent history of Europe and of Christianity.

The greatest new opportunity for Christians was that it finally became possible for all of the bishops of the Church to meet together in a big conference. After three centuries of smuggling letters to each other along slow international trade routes, the Church could now be organised in a much more straightforward, obvious and efficient way as one united institution, under the patronage of the Emperor.

There was much that needed to be discussed. In particular, the portrayal of Jesus in the four Gospels had described his character and actions very vividly, but left huge questions unanswered about his identity as one who seemed in some ways human and in some ways divine.[19] Some passages in the Gospels make Jesus sound equal to God the Father,[20] and some make him sound very human.[21] Various thinkers in the early centuries suggested some simple possible interpretations, seeing Jesus as an ordinary man in a uniquely close relationship with God, or as God disguised as a human being, or as a divine mind in a human body. But the Church rejected all of these as failing to do justice to the full witness of the Scriptures, condemning them as heresies.

The most popular alternative to the interpretation which finally prevailed is known to history as the heresy of Arianism, named after a priest in Alexandria called Arius (c. 256–336). He agreed that Jesus was far more exalted than the rest of creation, but thought that he was still a member of it. He thought that Jesus had been created at the beginning of time as the one through whom God then made everything else (his way of reading John 1). This made Jesus far superior to ordinary human beings, but inferior to God, like a sort of supreme angel, an intermediary between human beings and God.

In the year 325, the Emperor summoned the first ever council of all the bishops of the Church, in Nicaea (part of today's Turkey). About 300 attended. They condemned Arianism and established the view that Jesus was both fully divine and fully human. The verdict of that council forms the basis of the Nicene Creed, which is still used in worship today by Roman Catholics, Anglicans and Orthodox Christians, and is found in the official theologies of the main Protestant churches. It proclaims that Jesus was not created within time like us, but is eternally one with God the Father. He is 'God from God, Light from Light, true God of true God, begotten not made, of one Being with the Father.' And then that 'for us, and for our salvation, he came down from heaven, and was incarnate by the Holy Ghost of the Virgin Mary, and was made man.' Supporters of this Nicene theology, such as St Athanasius (c. 298 – 373), insisted both that Jesus needed to be fully divine in order to save us and to be worthy of worship, and also that Jesus needed to share fully in our human nature in order to save it. This is not a view explicitly

19   See Chapter 5 of *The Theology of Everything* for my account of Jesus' divine and human identity
20   e.g. John 1.1, 14.9, 20.28, Hebrews 1.3
21   e.g. Luke 2.40, Matthew 24.36, Mark 15.34

stated in the Bible, but Christians of all kinds ever since have mostly been content to see the Nicene Creed as the best way of doing justice to the complex picture of Jesus contained in the New Testament, ruling out all oversimplifications. Leading on to the doctrine of the Trinity (one God who is the three persons of Father, Son and Holy Spirit), it has formed the lens through which Christians read the Bible, dating from a time when the full contents of the Bible were still taking shape.

The Council of Nicaea thereby began a pattern of church government which has been very significant. When a controversial question needed to be settled, the bishops of the Church would meet together, pray, argue, discuss and sort it out. The main councils are called the 'Ecumenical Councils'. Seven were held in the first millennium, and they are recognised as divinely inspired and authoritative by Roman Catholics and by Orthodox Christians. The Roman Catholic Church has continued to function that way ever since. It has now reached a total of 21 councils, with the most recent being the Second Vatican Council of 1962-65.

Through the first councils and other discussions during the fourth and fifth centuries, final agreement was reached on the question of which books should be in the New Testament, and on further issues relating to the person of Christ and the doctrine of the Trinity. Christian doctrine became gradually more clearly defined, and various alternative approaches were ruled out as heresies.

Protestant theology today still incorporates some of the decisions made by those early bishops, but most Protestants are unaware of this and think that they are just following the obvious reading of the Bible.

PATRIARCHS AND POPES

Alongside these debates about Jesus, the early Church continued to develop its hierarchical systems of government. There were many bishops looking after local areas, but a small number of them came to develop a greater authority over wider areas, where they were in charge of the other bishops. The Council of Nicaea recognised that the bishops of Rome, Alexandria and Antioch had authority over wider areas, and Jerusalem and Constantinople later gained the same status.

During the sixth century, these five bishops gained the title of patriarchs, overseeing the patriarchates of Rome, Constantinople, Antioch, Jerusalem and Alexandria. Together, they covered most of the territory around the Mediterranean, including southern Europe, the Middle East and North Africa (including areas subsequently taken over by the development of Islam from the seventh century). The patriarchs mostly governed their own affairs within their own territories. But the bishop of Rome was understood to have the place of highest honour among them, and came to have the title Pope, meaning father.

European history progressed in a very different way in the patriarchate of Rome from the other four territories further east. The western Roman Empire fell to invading barbarians in the period around 410 AD, leaving the patriarch of Rome as a very significant cultural and political figure amidst the wreckage of western Roman civilisation. Meanwhile, the Roman Emperor had moved his headquarters east to Constantinople in 325 AD, where the Empire would continue for over a millennium (until the fall of Byzantium in 1453). The four patriarchates of Constantinople, Antioch, Jerusalem and Alexandria were very much under the Emperor's authority and protection. There was a cultural difference in this split between east and west: Rome spoke Latin, while the eastern patriarchates spoke Greek. So administrative, linguistic and social differences formed between the Christians of the east and the west.

Struggling valiantly amidst the chaos which surrounded it, the western church became very well-organised and focused. It began to be very successful in its mission to bring Christianity to the barbarian tribes who surrounded it in western Europe. King Ethelbert welcomed St Augustine[22] to Kent in 597, where he became the first Archbishop of Canterbury. On the continent, in 800, Pope Leo II crowned Charlemagne as Emperor over today's France and other nearby regions. The Pope gradually took on a leading role in the life of multiple countries in western Europe.

---

22   St Augustine of Canterbury, not to be confused with great early theologian St Augustine of
     Hippo (354-430), who is the Augustine I mention in various other places

As the patriarchate of Rome grew, so the theological understanding of the Papacy developed, based on a particular way of interpreting the Bible. The Pope was understood to be the successor of St Peter, who was believed to have been the first Bishop of Rome. And it was believed that Christ had given the leadership of the Church to Peter in order that he would pass it on to his successors as bishops of Rome. Jesus' words to Peter in the Gospels, calling him the rock on which he would build his Church,[23] were interpreted in that light. The popes therefore began to claim more and more authority over the rest of the Church, including the Greek-speaking territory to the east.

But these claims to universal jurisdiction were never formally recognised by the eastern patriarchs. Constantinople, Antioch, Jerusalem and Alexandria were proud of their own historic traditions and were never willing to accept the Pope as more than the first among equals, the patriarch of greatest honour. The Christian faiths of the east and the west continued to grow apart over a long period, for political and cultural reasons. The division became formal and final in the year 1054 in the event known as the Great Schism. Following a row over the authority of Rome, both sides excommunicated the other. Despite various attempts to heal the rift, they have remained divided ever since.

These four eastern patriarchates are the origins of the Orthodox Churches of today, while the western patriarchate is what we now know as the Roman Catholic Church. As I have described, the main thing they fell out over was the authority of the Pope, who is ironically meant to be a focus of Christian unity. But Orthodox theologians also get very annoyed about one extra word which western Christians had inserted in the Nicene Creed: *filioque,* meaning 'and the Son'. Without the filioque, the Creed says that the Holy Spirit proceeds from the Father, thereby neatly presenting the Father alone as the eternal source both of the Son and the Spirit. With the filioque added, the Creed now says that the Holy Spirit proceeds from the Father *and the Son,* establishing a less symmetrical set of relationships.[24] The procession of the

---

23   Matthew 16.18-19

24   John 15.26 describes the Son's role in sending the Spirit into the world, so the debate concerns whether this event is a revelation of the eternal origins of the Spirit

Spirit was a lively debate in the first millennium but is one which most western theologians have lost interest in, an apathy which annoys the Orthodox even more.

From a Protestant perspective, Orthodox and Catholic theology and spirituality have much in common. Both groups attach great importance to their established hierarchy of bishops, priests and deacons and its continuity through the whole of Christian history. They value beautiful sacred buildings, elaborate ceremonies and traditional liturgies. They ask for the prayers of saints whom they believe are in heaven, venerating especially Mary as the Mother of God. They pray for the souls of others who have died, and they place a great emphasis on seven sacraments in the life of the Church. They have well-developed traditions of religious orders, in which communities of monks and nuns live under vows of poverty, chastity and obedience. These are all aspects of Christian faith which developed during the first millennium, which I shall say more about in the next two chapters.

A HIERARCHICAL CHRISTIAN SOCIETY

In the centuries following the Great Schism of 1054, the Roman Catholic Church consolidated its power and wealth in western Europe. In 1302, Pope Boniface VIII declared that 'it is absolutely necessary for the salvation of every human creature to be subject to the Roman Pontiff.' The Catholic vision at the time was of a united Christian society in which everyone understood their place in a hierarchical structure. The church hierarchy ran alongside a fixed social and political hierarchy which it supported: popes and archbishops crowned kings, and kings presided over an agricultural society in which the aristocracy owned the land and the peasants worked in the fields. By this time, bishops were themselves aristocrats living in palaces, looked after by many servants and occasionally even with their own private armies. Knights built parish churches as well as their own castles and manor houses, and often installed their younger sons as priests.[25]

---

25   See Chapter 1 of *The Theology of Everything* for more about this hierarchical view of reality, and its contrast with other systems

This was a very stable society, in which there was considerable technological and economic growth. The first universities were founded at this time, as Catholic institutions with papal charters. But there was no concept of religious freedom at this time, just as there was no concept of democracy. All people were baptised as infants and brought up as Catholics, with the only exceptions being the minority communities of Jews, who endured episodes of persecution and expulsion. The Crusades united soldiers from countries across western Europe to resist the expansion of Islamic rule in formerly Christian territory, as well as fighting against pagan tribes and Christian heretics.

The Protestant and atheist propaganda of recent centuries presents this as a very dark and fearful time, in which all lived in fear of being tortured by the Inquisition. But those who are more sympathetic to Catholicism have admired the extraordinary architecture of the cathedrals and churches of that era and the beauty of their decorations. It seems to many to have been a very vibrant and inventive society, known also through stories of brave knights, chivalry and colourful heraldry.

People then would have thought that it was obvious that things were the way they were because God had made them that way. They mostly accepted whatever position in the world they were born into, obeyed those in authority, and often found that the roles given to them were very meaningful and rewarding. Atheism was largely unknown and would have seemed ridiculous to most. People accepted that the Catholic faith was true in the same kind of way that people today accept that physical exercise is good for our health: no one credible disputed it seriously, but the degree to which individuals took it to heart varied greatly, from apathy to fanatical enthusiasm.

The Middle Ages are the high-point of a unified hierarchical society, in which a top-down view of the Catholic Church fitted seamlessly into an aristocratic system of government. God reigned on high as the source of all earthly hierarchies, through which his power and glory descended. Bishops ordained priests who brought the holy sacraments and teachings of the Church to lay people, hearing their confessions and proclaiming God's forgiveness. Kings ruled over the nobility, who were in charge of those who worked on their lands. At every level of society, the good life was understood to involve participating in the divine grace brought down by those higher up, responding with due humility, respect and obedience to God and all of his representatives. I shall say more about this hierarchical vision of divine grace and human participation in the next chapter.

This entire social order was understood to have been established from on high by God for the good of all. Within it, all the teachings and ceremonies of the Church were believed to be divinely inspired and infallible. It was a very impressive system, but the power and wealth amassed by the Church presented a problem to the authenticity of its faith.

Christian ministry had originally carried a strong chance of following Jesus to an early martyrdom, but now it was a ticket to a very privileged life. Not surprisingly, the higher ranks of the Church attracted leaders who were sometimes scandalously immoral, holding those positions out of their own ambitions for money and power. Their lives could be a long way from the example of Jesus – the one who had washed his disciples' feet and told them that the greatest among them would be their servant.[26]

Lots of different tensions developed in the later Middle Ages. Populations and economies had grown, and individual monarchs were becoming more powerful and were flexing their national military muscles. Theologians were looking closely at the Bible and the writings of the early Church fathers, enjoying the advances in scholarship brought by the medieval universities. Devout Christians were sometimes shocked by the state of the Church and its leaders. The invention of the printing press by Gutenberg in 1440 made it much easier for radical thinkers to share and spread ideas. It became less and less easy for one central authority to keep a hold on what everybody was thinking and teaching. The top-down hierarchical system finally broke open in the 16th century at the Reformation.

26   John 13.1-20, Mark 10.35-45

THE REFORMATION AND
THE BIRTH OF PROTESTANTISM

The final trigger for revolution was the practice known as the sale of indulgences. The Church was raising money for the building of St Peter's Basilica in Rome by selling documents which claimed to reduce people's time of suffering after death in purgatory (a subject I will return to in the next two chapters). In other words, the Catholic Church was selling places on an alleged fast track to heaven. This was a step too far: how could this be an authentic development and interpretation of the teachings of Jesus Christ? The founder of Christianity had said, 'Blessed are you who are poor, for yours is the kingdom of God... But woe to you who are rich, for you have received your consolation.'[27] He had not said, 'Blessed are you who are rich, for you will have the necessary funds to buy your way into paradise.' And if the Church had gone so badly astray on this subject, motivated by the desire to further increase its own wealth and splendour, then how else had it betrayed Jesus, and how many more of its teachings were not divinely inspired after all?

A German monk and theologian called Martin Luther (1483-1546) began a protest against the sale of indulgences in 1517, by nailing his famous Ninety-Five Theses to the door of the Church in Wittenberg. Luther had been through his own personal struggle with Catholic teachings and spirituality, as I will describe in the next chapter. Reading the Bible, especially Paul's letters to the Romans and the Galatians, he had found an emphasis on the grace of God as a free gift, received through faith. He was appalled that people were being told that they needed to pay the Church in order to avoid the pains of divine judgement.

Luther established the new Protestant emphasis on justification by faith alone, which I will also explore in more detail in the next chapter. He said that salvation is all about something which Jesus Christ has done for us. Because of Jesus' life, death and resurrection, God is willing to see us as righteous. God forgives us and accepts us because of

27 Luke 6.20,24

Jesus Christ, not because of our achievements, or our donations to the Church or our busy devotion to Catholic ceremonies.

This belief in justification by faith alone was based on Luther's reading of the Bible, not on the traditional Catholic interpretation of the Scriptures. He concluded that the Church could go very seriously wrong, and that popes and councils of bishops could make grave mistakes. For Luther, there was an urgent need to go back to the documents which recorded the beginnings of Christianity, seeking to read the Bible with fresh eyes and to bring reform to the Church.

Tragically, the Church hierarchy failed to engage constructively with Luther's criticisms of the scandal of indulgences. Luther was excommunicated by the Pope in 1521, and so began the separate existence of factions which protested against the errors of Rome: the Protestants.

Before Luther, the Catholics had emphasised that the Bible should only be read by the professionals. They were confident that they knew the correct way of interpreting it, which was understood by the clergy and taught to the laity. They were sure that only the Church's tradition gave the correct approach to the Scriptures. This is the top-down approach to Christian faith which had prevailed for many centuries. But Luther's approach began to open up the possibility that ordinary people could read the Bible for themselves, without being constrained by the traditional Catholic way of making sense of it. His achievements included the translation of the New Testament into German, which was printed in large numbers from 1522. This was soon followed by William Tyndale's version in English in 1526.

PROTESTANT DIVERSITY

One of the great slogans of the Reformation is *Sola Scriptura*, meaning 'the Bible alone'. It proclaims that the Scriptures are the one authoritative source of Christian doctrine, and that they must stand above all traditions and all the deductions of human reason. This belief is still a key feature of the conservative Evangelical corner of my diagram. The Reformers believed that they could return to a purer form of Christianity, cleansed from the Catholic traditions which had led the medieval Church astray, and rescued from the influence of too

much pagan Greek philosophy. They valued some of the writings of
the early theologians, such as St Augustine, and the creeds of the early
Church, but only because they seemed to be reliable guides to the true
content of the Scriptures.

However, the Bible itself is a library of many different texts from
many times and genres. Finding a way through them to an interpretation of their message is not a straightforward task. If we announce that
we will now just believe the Bible, this does not immediately settle the
matter of the content of Christian doctrine. Luther's approach was to
present his doctrine of justification by faith as the heart of the true message of the Scriptures, seeing it therefore as the key to the interpretation
of the whole Bible so that everything else was read in that light. I see
this as the inauguration of a new tradition of understanding the Bible,
rather than the removal of tradition.[28] In fact, it was the inauguration
of a new family of traditions of understanding the Bible, because they
soon began to diversify.

The great weakness of Protestantism is that Luther's approach
did not just result in one united biblical Church. The Protestants very
quickly began to disagree with each other about the details of how to
understand the Bible. Previously, there had been one theology which
was established by the medieval Church, and which people assumed
had all been revealed by the Holy Spirit. Now, any individual or group
could develop their own theology, and that was increasingly what
they did.

After a while there were Lutherans, and Calvinists, and Anglicans,
and then there were the Puritans, and Congregationalists, and Baptists, and Presbyterians, and Ranters and Quakers and lots of other
kinds of Protestants. All of them tended to be convinced that their way
of reading the Bible was the correct one and that everyone else was
being wilfully stupid. Some of their disagreements were about things
like sacraments and worship, which I will return to in the next two
chapters. But the thing that Protestants have disagreed most about is
the subject of this chapter: how to understand and organise churches.
As I described at the beginning, the Bible does not clearly answer this

28   See pp. 79-84 for further discussion of the strengths and weaknesses of this approach

question. So, if we abandon the traditions that developed from the second century onwards, we are not left with any detailed instructions.

PROTESTANTISM AND ESTABLISHMENT

To begin with, Luther and other early Reformers assumed that Christianity would still be a top-down system, and that the Church would still be in a close alliance with the state. Their ideal society was not a democratic one in which people made up their own minds about religion. Instead, they hoped for a good Protestant king who would impose true biblical Christianity on all his people, wisely knowing what was best for them.

Across Europe, both Protestants and Catholics wanted their version of Christianity to be the established, state religion. A whole country or principality would be understood to hold that faith. All infants would be baptised, all children would be taught the faith, and everyone would be expected to go to church on Sundays and other holy days.

But the idea of a Christian country is not mentioned in the New Testament, which was written by Christians who were a minority in a world ruled by others. The idea of a Christian country is more reminiscent of the situation of Israel in the Old Testament, when the whole Jewish race and nation were seen as the people of God. But was that model still appropriate for Christianity? An increasing number of Protestants thought that it was not. And so there came also a more radical approach to reformation which turned its attention to the ordinary people and their faith, rather than to monarchies and hierarchies.

The first flourishing of this new radicalism came in a group called the Anabaptists. They began as a small minority in Germany, where they were regarded as dangerous lunatics by everybody else, a point of view which did at least give Catholics and most other Protestants something to agree about. Anabaptists wanted the separation of Church and state, believing that a ruler could not impose true Christianity on all people. They said that infant baptism was invalid as they could find no mention of it the Bible, and that baptism was for adults who could declare their own decision to follow Jesus Christ. Their name refers to 'baptising again', since they would rebaptise those who had been christened as babies.

Anabaptists thought that the Reformation was not going far enough. They emphasised the priesthood of all believers,[29] rather than a special group of ordained clergy. They went further than anyone else in looking at the Church from the ground upwards, emphasising that all Christians could be guided by the Holy Spirit and could read the Bible for themselves.

This was the beginnings of the discovery that there can be something inherently democratic in a Protestant approach to Christianity. The Protestant way of trusting the laity with the Bible can lead to radicalism, giving ordinary people the tools to reimagine the world and to set about trying to change it.

The history of Protestant churches and the history of the development of Western democracy are therefore deeply interconnected, especially in England and its colonies. However, this was not at all apparent at the beginning. When the English Church broke away from the Roman Catholic Church, it retained its hierarchical structure and placed it under the full authority of the English monarchy. The English Church preserved intact its branch of the Catholic system of archbishops, bishops, priests and deacons, so that its clergy continued working with the same ecclesiastical titles in the same parish churches and cathedrals. It merely said that the Pope had no jurisdiction in England, and that the monarch was now the Supreme Governor instead. The aim was for the Church of England to continue as the Church for all people in the country, baptising all infants and holding together everyone in this one faith.

Especially from the reign of Elizabeth I (1558-1603) onwards, the Church of England made a serious attempt to unite as many people as possible in this one national Church, from those who remembered the old Catholic liturgies with warm nostalgia to those who longed for a more radical revolution. This was never entirely possible, and religious diversity became increasingly apparent.

29   1 Peter 2.5, 9

In the sixteenth and seventeenth centuries, enthusiastic reformers known as Puritans tried hard to purge the Church of England of its remaining Catholic tendencies. Some of them gave up and set up separatist congregations. Some of them went to the new English colonies in America, such as the famous Pilgrim Fathers in 1620, where they gained the freedom to practice their own approaches to Christianity. In Scotland, Presbyterians got rid of bishops and ran the church through democratic councils of presbyters (the middle of the original three orders of ministers). Congregationalists went even further, forming independent churches which were governed democratically by all their members. Baptists got started in England soon afterwards, being Congregationalists who rejected infant baptism. Thomas Helwys wrote in 1612: 'Men's religion to God is betwixt God and themselves; the King shall not answer for it.' Some new Protestant groups were pacifists, notably the Quakers. Others sought a violent revolution, and so there was a civil war in England, and a period without a king from 1649-1660.

By the end of the 17th century, England had a restored monarchy whose powers were carefully limited by Parliament, which was elected by a few percent of the wealthiest English land-owning men. It had a Church of England which was established, but people were no longer persecuted if they chose to adopt their own approach to Protestantism. Congregationalists, Presbyterians, Baptists and others became a more settled part of the English landscape, as also in America, growing through the 18th century.

Increasingly, a Protestant approach to Christianity was associated with a stubborn independence rather than a deference to established authorities and aristocratic leaders. The American Declaration of Independence of 1776, rejecting the remaining authority of the British monarchy, includes this famous statement:

> We hold these truths to be self-evident, that all men are created equal, that they are endowed by their Creator with certain unalienable Rights, that among these are Life, Liberty and the pursuit of Happiness.

This is a decisive affirmation of human rights and freedoms, based on a Protestant theology which offers a bottom-up view of God's creation. In this view, God works by providing a space in which people are free to pursue happiness for themselves, rather than by imposing a hierarchical system in which order and meaning are handed down to us by our superiors.

EVANGELICALISM

Ideas about human liberty were advancing, both in European society and within Protestant churches at this time. The Roman Catholic Church continued to oppose freedom of religion until the Second Vatican Council (1962-5), maintaining the historic view that a good Christian state would not allow any alternatives to the one true faith. But liberty was a very significant theme within the Evangelical movement, which began in the 18th century and flourished especially in Britain and America. In England, it was especially associated with John Wesley (1703-1791), the founder of the Methodists. Evangelicals moved completely away from the old assumption that a king would establish a religion for all of his people. Instead, they placed a great emphasis on the need for individual conversion, the need for each person to make his or her own decision to follow Jesus Christ with a genuine and heartfelt faith.

Methodism was an enormously popular movement, which spread very fast among ordinary people on both sides of the Atlantic through the 18th and 19th centuries. Wesley himself was a priest in the Church of England and always intended to remain so, but his movement rapidly outgrew all traditional structures, before eventually settling down as a new Protestant denomination. Evangelical revivals were marked by vast outdoor meetings where crowds responded to the enthusiastic preaching of the Gospel.

This was the time when the Industrial Revolution was beginning to bring huge changes to society, uprooting large numbers of workers from old farming villages to new factories in rapidly-growing towns and cities. In America, it was the era when European settlers moved west across huge new territories, pioneering their own new ways of life. Within all of this upheaval, Evangelical Christianity offered people a sense of morality and community, along with the confidence that God was working through them as they explored the challenges of a world which was now changing rapidly.

Evangelical Christianity developed a very entrepreneurial and creative approach, in which preachers could gather congregations and establish churches in fast-growing settlements. The old top-down approach was much less adaptable and was deeply negligent in its response to new opportunities. Remarkably, Anglicans in the United States were not even given their own bishops until 1784, a century after the colonies of New England began. Back in England, the response to the growth of industrial urban areas was also very slow. Church building had from the Middle Ages been the role of land-owning aristocrats, financed by a tithe on agricultural produce, so there was no established system for setting up new parish churches in fast-growing cities. The grass-roots popularism of the Evangelical movement was quicker to engage with the ambitions of the new middle classes and the needs of the urban poor. Protestantism flourished and diversified through this period.

Social change and social action were part of Evangelicalism from the beginning. Its context was a drastic move away from the kind of settled social structures which were so familiar to the authors of the New Testament and to the people of medieval Europe. The Evangelical emphasis on the right and responsibility of all individuals to make their own choices about faith was associated with a belief in liberty which went far beyond anything known to the writers of the Bible.

It was Evangelical Christians such as William Wilberforce (1759-1833) who led the way in campaigning for an end to slavery in the British Empire, a campaign which succeeded in the last year of his life.[30] From our perspective, that was the ending of an evil, the removal of a departure from the way things should be. But it was also part of the formation of a new kind of social order, in which freedom for everyone was cherished far more than ever before, and now regarded as a God-given right.

30   See pp. 143-150 for further discussion of the abolition of slavery

The New Testament had said that slaves should obey their masters[31] and that God had instituted the governing authorities of the world.[32] Throughout most of Christian history, the leaders of the Church had assumed that God worked by getting people to know their place in society and to obey hierarchies. For most of this time, the prevailing view had been that God had given to kings and lords the role of establishing churches within very stable societies. But now Evangelical Christianity flourished through the discovery that people could respond much more directly to the message of the Gospel as individuals within a fast-changing world.

In this sense, Evangelicalism inherently involves one step in a liberal direction away from the most conservative corner on my diagram. It depends on the view that something godly was being uncovered in the social changes associated with a growing belief in liberty. It is a move away from unthinking deference to tradition. But Evangelicalism has subsequently often been nervous of further social changes, such as the opening up of male roles to women or the opening up of marriage to same-sex couples, worrying that those changes go against the Bible. In America, large-scale Evangelical interventions in politics in recent decades have meanwhile made others very nervous about the obstructive power of Evangelical movements. Chapters Five, Six and Seven will explore those tensions further.

The creativity of Evangelicalism has also sometimes been a problem. Without any form of discipline from an established hierarchy, Evangelical Christianity has also spilled over into various new movements and cults which have abandoned core Christian doctrines, especially the Trinity, or have added on new scriptures. These are people who read the Bible enthusiastically, but whose interpretation of it is now too different from the historic Christian faith to be compatible with it. The most famous examples are the Mormons and the Jehovah's Witnesses, all of whom see themselves as the true followers of God's revelation in the Bible. An enthusiasm for predicting the date of the end of the

31   Ephesians 6.5
32   Romans 13.1-3

world is a feature of some of these offshoots,[33] and of some who have remained otherwise more conventionally Evangelical.

As seen in the enthusiasm of their early revival meetings, many Evangelical groups have placed a strong emphasis on individual supernatural experiences of the Holy Spirit. And that has led to the Pentecostal and Charismatic movements which have spread very rapidly around the world since the early 20th century. Pentecostal and Charismatic Christians emphasise the miraculous work of the Holy Spirit in individuals and in local churches: leading to prophecies, healings, speaking in tongues, and a style of worship which is informal, spontaneous and joyful. Pentecostalism has grown very quickly in the southern hemisphere, especially in communities affected by poverty, and often where Catholicism has been associated with wealth and privilege.

Protestantism has from the beginning eroded the Catholic emphasis on clergy, monks and nuns as religious professionals whose vocation sets them apart from all others. The Charismatic movement's emphasis on the guidance of the Holy Spirit has an especially strong focus on 'every member ministry': the idea that God gives all Christians a variety of natural and supernatural abilities to enable them to serve him in the local church.

RELIGIOUS FREEDOM AND DIVERSITY IN BRITAIN

Protestant religious diversity expanded in Britain during the 18th and 19th centuries, often connected with the new wealth and social structures created by the Industrial Revolution. While the traditions of the Church of England had often involved aristocratic landowners and their farm labourers, the industrialists and merchants of the new middle classes frequently preferred to establish themselves as leading members of new non-conformist Protestant churches.

From the late-17th until the mid-19th centuries, this kind of dissent was tolerated, but carried disadvantages. People who were not practising members of the Church of England, supporting its teachings and

---

33 Jesus warned against this sort of thing – see for example Mark 13.32 – but enthusiasts have often still searched the rest of the Scriptures for clues

taking communion at least annually, were barred from various influential positions in the life of England, Wales and Ireland. For example,
they could not be Members of Parliament, or magistrates, or army
officers, or even go to university. Universities were solidly Anglican
institutions, where matriculation required a declaration of assent to
the 39 Articles of the Church of England. In this way, dissenters were
no longer regarded as criminals, but were seen as too suspicious to be
trusted with any real influence.

As the middle-class Evangelical non-conformists got increasingly
numerous, wealthy, and generous in their philanthropic donations, and
as the life of the nation was dominated more by industry and global
trade than by agriculture, their marginalisation began to seem increasingly odd. A series of reforms centred on the period from the 1830s to
1870s opened up all areas of national life regardless of religious affili-
ation. Methodists, Baptists, Catholics, Jews and others began to study
at Oxford and Cambridge and to be elected to the House of Commons.

This huge increase in religious freedom removed most of the power
of the Church of England. It was completely disestablished in Ireland
and Wales. In England, it retained only some of the trappings of estab-
lishment, and the process began of removing its traditional income from
the agricultural tithe. Facing these challenges, it thought more deeply
about its true religious roots. The result was the two great religious
revivals which greatly enriched its life and continue to shape it today,
coming from both ends of the low-to-high scale.

The first revival came simply from the way that the Church of
England was itself greatly influenced by Evangelicalism. John Wesley
himself was a Church of England priest, and his ministry inspired many
Anglicans. Evangelical missionary societies, theological colleges, newspapers, hymns, networks and campaigning groups grew and flourished.

More surprisingly, another movement then appeared, enriching
the higher end of the Church. High churchmanship in the Church of
England had previously rested on the idea that this was the Church
of the English monarch and the state, holding a dazzlingly privileged
status in the life of the nation. But now the old elite institutions were
opening up to everyone, and Parliament was still growing in power,

and there were even MPs from other religious groups who could vote on how the Church of England should be run. This was intolerable for clergy who had enjoyed their unique status in the old English hierarchy.

The answer was to emphasise the other hierarchy: the ecclesiastical hierarchy which had been inherited from the Roman Catholic Church and which went back right to the beginnings of Christianity. Suddenly, high-church Anglicans became very interested in the apostolic succession of bishops, and the idea that Church of England priests had inherited through their bishops an authenticity and sacramental power which all other Protestants had lost.[34] This viewpoint grew through the Oxford Movement from 1833, and then was more widely known as Anglo-Catholicism. Anglo-Catholics spoke of the true Catholic Church as having three branches: the Orthodox, the Roman Catholics and the Anglicans, each preserving the true apostolic succession of bishops and their divinely-given authority. Anglo-Catholics thought that their clergy had received the same powers as Roman Catholic priests to turn bread and wine into the body and blood of Christ, setting them far above the ministers of Methodist, Baptist and other Protestant Churches, whom they looked down on as mere laymen without valid ordinations. It must be noted that the Roman Catholics and the Orthodox Churches have never signed up to this high view of Anglicans. Indeed, Pope Leo XIII pronounced in 1896 that ordinations of Anglican clergy were 'absolutely null and utterly void', just like those of other Protestant ministers. Nevertheless, the Anglo-Catholic movement continued to grow during the early decades of the 20th century.

Anglo-Catholics saw the Reformation as a tragedy rather than a triumph, and began to restore many of the ceremonies and traditions abandoned in the 16th century. The revival of elaborate and beautiful rituals was interconnected with a widespread Victorian nostalgia for neogothic architecture and medieval art, as seen in the many new churches of the time. Anglo-Catholics in turn set up their own theological colleges, missionary societies, newspapers, hymns, networks and campaigning groups, arguing with the Evangelical ones.

---

34   See Chapter Three for more about Catholic and Protestant views of the sacraments

The result was a very diverse Church of England which in some places was theologically very similar to the Methodists and Presbyterians, and in other places was very similar to the Roman Catholics. Trying to preserve the peace were the 'broad church' people in the middle who found some things to admire in both groups. This, as I described in the first chapter, is what has provided my very congenial ecclesiastical home.

TWO VIEWS OF MINISTRY

As a result of this diverse history, Christian ministry is seen from two very different perspectives within the Church of England. To describe them, here are two imaginary but realistic examples of today's local churches.

My first example is a big Evangelical parish church, which has a staff team including a vicar,[35] a youth worker and an administrator. Various members of the congregation also often help to preach, lead services, provide pastoral care or lead Bible study groups. Its low-church perspective is very pragmatic, describing people in terms of job descriptions, avoiding making much of a distinction between clergy and laity. The vicar wears the same sort of smartish casual clothing as the others (even during services), and all are known by their first names. They are admired primarily for the ability they have to explain the Gospel and to show the love of Christ to others. The fact that the vicar is ordained as a priest is hardly ever mentioned, but the congregation values the deep knowledge of the Bible that he shows in his long sermons. The church has very strong relationships with local Evangelical churches from other denominations, but most of the congregation would not be able to remember the name of the diocesan bishop.

Meanwhile, at the Anglo-Catholic parish on the other side of the town, the vicar is always seen in a clerical collar and often in robes, and is usually addressed as 'Father'. The fact that he is a priest who

---

35   Adding further to the complexity, *vicar* is not one of those many biblical titles I mentioned earlier. It originally meant a priest who *vicariously* looked after a parish church on behalf of the rector (the person who was entitled to receive the income from the local agricultural tithe). That financial arrangement is long gone, but vicar has remained as the most popular title for a Church of England parish priest.

has been ordained by a bishop in the true apostolic succession of the Catholic Church is seen as absolutely vital, giving him the power to preside over valid sacraments, especially the daily celebrations of the Mass. The high-church perspective sees his ministry as a state of being which was imparted at ordination, when he was set apart from other people to inhabit this sacred role. This sense of the priest as a special person helps to emphasise that church services are holy occasions, full of awe and transcendent beauty, different from ordinary life. A big fuss is made of the diocesan bishop when he visits, and the fact that the Church of England preserves the historic threefold ministry of bishops, priests and deacons is seen as essential. Members of this church avoid using the title Protestant to describe themselves: they think that the neighbouring Protestant churches do not have validly ordained clergy and that Christ does not become physically present in the bread and wine of their inferior and infrequent communion services. They feel they have more in common with the Roman Catholics and the Orthodox and have sometimes thought about joining them.

Those two very different visions of Christian ministry coexist in the same Church, sometimes very fruitfully and sometimes rather uneasily. Bishops do all they can to keep the peace between the different factions, rather than imposing a single vision from on high. Meanwhile, the Church of England as a whole has become much more democratic. Significant decisions are made by an elected General Synod, which includes lay-people, priests and bishops. All three groups have to agree by a two-thirds majority on any major changes. Within each diocese, an elected Diocesan Synod shares with the local bishop the administration of that region's churches.

CONCLUSION:
COMBINING THE BEST OF THE HIGH AND THE LOW

The diversity of high and low churches within the Church of England reflects something of the even greater diversity of Catholicism, Orthodoxy and Protestantism around the world, which combine imperfectly to form a global community unlike any other. As the world's largest faith, Christianity contains more people than the largest country or corporation. It connects people of many languages and ethnic groups from all around the world, from all levels of society, from all educational backgrounds and all levels of wealth. Inevitably this vast set of networks has many tensions and family feuds, some of which feature in this book. But it is a work of grace that holds this complex web of relationships together. Bonds of prayer, friendship and practical support stretch across continents and denominations, bringing people together who would otherwise have nothing in common.

As I have described, Christians have looked at this structure from two directions, and both have their strengths and weaknesses. From the middle ground, it is possible to try to identify the best of both.

The low-church approach is very adaptable and responsive to local circumstances, empowering ordinary people to build Christian community together, exploring their vocations and developing their gifts in God's service. But it runs the risk of fragmenting into little groups over minor disagreements, or of having no accountability when separate groups go wildly astray. Even without the grand robes and titles, some low-church clergy still nurture an inflated sense of their own importance, which can be all the more dangerous when there is no bishop to keep an eye on them or to deal with complaints.

The high-church approach is often much more deeply-rooted in traditional wisdom, with careful structures that are designed to guard against problems and errors. It is less likely to chase after the changing fashions of the world, and better at communicating a sense of the holiness of the Church. But its privileged hierarchies can be too slow to notice the needs of ordinary congregations, or too slow to acknowledge works of the Spirit which arise from a local level. Its insistence on the essential importance of valid ordinations is called into question by the many examples of excellent Protestant ministers who have not been ordained by bishops but whose ministry is obviously Spirit-filled and fruitful.

When trying to bring the best of those two approaches together, I find it helpful to think again about the three orders of ministry set up in the early Church. It seems to me that they are found in some form far more widely than just among those churches which preserve an apostolic succession of bishops. Among high and low denominations around the globe, good Christian ministry does usually seem to operate on three scales.

Working in the middle scale are those known to Catholics, Orthodox and Anglicans as priests, but also known as presbyters, ministers, pastors, vicars, chaplains, and various other titles among Protestants. In some form, they are almost universal among denominations. It is normal for each local church of any kind to have a leader, someone who takes the main responsibility for preaching, leading services, providing pastoral care for the congregation and representing that church to the community around it. A good leader will nurture the gifts of the congregation, and encourage them as they share these tasks with the church, and as they live out their faith in their daily lives.

Under the authority of the priest/presbyter/pastor/minister, the narrowest scale is the domain of those traditionally known to Catholics, Orthodox and Anglicans as deacons. But deacons are a source of great misunderstanding in high churches, since few of those formally ordained to that role now exist. Despite a renewal of interest in recent decades, there are still not many in those denominations who are deacons permanently. In the Church of England, they are normally in training to be priests, and they remain deacons for only a year. As deacons, they may use the title 'Reverend', wear clerical collars, and take part in leading services and preaching, but they do not yet preside at communion services or give blessings. Their duties only partly resemble the practical assistance given by deacons in the early Church, such as distributing food to widows,[36] even if they are ordained in the same sort of way.

Meanwhile, local churches often do have lay-people who are exercising various official ministries with a narrower focus under the leadership of the priest/presbyter/pastor/minister. They might be taking communion to the housebound, visiting those who are ill, helping to preach and lead services, running Bible study groups or teaching the Christian faith to children. In the Church of England, such people may be called Readers, Licenced Lay Ministers, Authorised Lay Ministers,

36 Acts 6.1-6

Lay Workers, Church Wardens or various other titles, and other denominations have their equivalents. This seems to me to be the real third layer of Christian ministry, the true diaconate. The interesting thing is that it has arisen from the ground up under a wide variety of circumstances, and is completely disconnected from the high-church belief in ordained deacons as people who have been transformed into clergy by the prayers of a bishop. Every good church should have a number of authorised lay ministers of some kind, supporting the work of the priest/presbyter/pastor/minister. And this is just what seems to happen spontaneously in flourishing churches of most kinds. Many higher churches struggle unnecessarily if they leave too many tasks to be done by an overworked priest.

Looking in the other direction, the widest scale of Christian ministry is the sphere of those known to Catholics, Orthodox and Anglicans as bishops. I have described how those churches value this historic ministry very highly. But again, I would suggest that there is more going on in this sphere than is immediately obvious. The ministry of oversight has evolved beyond just bishops even in those historic churches, and has become present in other forms among many Protestants.

In the Church of England, the traditional power of the episcopate has been more widely distributed by democratic systems of synods which also involve lay people and priests. Moreover, the task of looking after many churches across a whole region is not just undertaken by bishops. They share that role with archdeacons (who, very confusingly, are technically actually priests), area deans (also priests), and various lay people such as safeguarding officers and diocesan secretaries.

In other forms of Protestantism which do not have bishops, something resembling episcopacy often tends to evolve, at least to some extent. Most churches will tend to join forces in ways which involve some systems of accountability, oversight and mutual support between congregations across wider areas, led by named individuals or committees. This seems to me to be genuinely episcopal, even when those roles have developed from the ground up rather than fitting the top-down model of the apostolic succession of bishops.

When groups of churches function well, ministers in episcopal-type roles also have a regard for ecumenical relationships which stretch between denominations and around the world. They nurture supportive links and constructive dialogues, which continue the concern for the well-being of the whole Christian Church that was shown by the bishops in the councils of the early Church. Many lower churches struggle unnecessarily if they prefer to function in isolation, without enjoying this sense of being supported by the whole global Church.

In this episcopal-level nurturing of helpful relationships, there is a careful balance to get right. The Roman Catholic Church errs on the side of giving too much power to the Vatican at the top, maintaining its vast structure by insisting on its infallibility and avoiding any official admission of its errors. Protestants tend to err on the side of being too fragmented, forming yet another split when their opinions diverge again. The Anglican Communion tries, I think, to take a very valuable middle way in this respect: staying together as much as possible, while being honest about our differences and struggles.

And so I conclude that the Church should be understood both from the top down and from the bottom up. Its bishops are important, seeking the wellbeing of the Church across wide areas and global communities. And the ministries of its lay people are vital, including those who might have been called deacons in the early Church. I support the high-church belief that healthy Christianity involves the traditional three orders of Christian ministry operating on those three different scales, although I think that high churches usually misunderstand and undervalue the true diaconate. And, sharing a lower-church perspective, I am happy to affirm that such ministries often spring up locally from the work of the Holy Spirit within individual congregations, rather than always descending tidily and triumphantly through the historic apostolic succession of bishops.

From my central perspective, I think that the grand, global view of the Church should be held carefully in tension with the humble and local view. I support the Catholic belief that the history of the Church as a set of institutions guided by God is significant and meaningful, that its shared traditions should be valued and should never be discarded without good reason, and that a concern for visible unity on a global scale is important. But, supporting a Protestant perspective, I do think that the Church is often in need of reformation: it can be led astray by a human ambition for power and worldly glory which gets too comfortable within grand ecclesiastical structures. Any hierarchy must be willing to admit its fallibility and must always remember that it exists to serve and support local churches. In the next two chapters, I will continue to explore how to keep those high and low perspectives in balance.

In this chapter, I have discussed the variations in forms of church government which can be the most obvious set of wide variations between denominations. But the difference between the top-down and bottom-up approaches goes deeper than that, providing contrasting visions of the nature of salvation itself. That is the subject of the next chapter.

SUGGESTIONS FOR FURTHER READING

For an overview of Church history, I recommend *A History of Christianity: The First Three Thousand Years* by Diarmaid MacCulloch (2010, Penguin).

The early development of Church hierarchies can be seen in some of the texts collected and translated by Andrew Louth and Maxwell Staniforth in *Early Christian Writings: The Apostolic Fathers* (1987, Penguin Classics).

For later texts which show the rise of a bottom-up view of the Church, see *Radical Christian Writings: A Reader* edited by Andrew Bradstock and Christopher Rowland (2009, John Wiley & Sons).

Chapter Three
Knowing God's Grace: Sacraments and Faith

CATHOLICISM:
TRANSFORMATION IN THIS LIFE AND AFTERWARDS

There are so many differences between the details of Protestantism and Catholicism that it is easy to get lost in them. But underlying most of them is just one single factor: a contrast between two visions of salvation.

Here again, the Catholic vision is top-down: it focuses on a destination which is far above, and a hierarchical system which descends to meet us as we participate in it. In this framework, salvation is the journey of the soul upwards to heaven, where it will be united with God in a state of perfect bliss. The ascent involves a long process of transformation, in which individuals are cleansed first from the guilt of the original sin of Adam and then of their own subsequent sins, growing in love, holiness and virtue, losing all unhealthy attachments, and drawing gradually closer to God. It is usually the case that this process is not completed in this life, but is brought to perfection after death during a period of time in purgatory (perhaps of many thousands of years), until the soul is finally ready for heaven.

This spiritual ascent is enabled by the grace of God flowing down to meet us. In particular, that grace descends through the sacraments of the Church, which God gives us in order to make our journey possible.

The seven sacraments are:

- **Baptism** (popularly known as Christening)
- **The Eucharist** (the Mass, which is known to Protestants as Holy Communion or the Lord's Supper)
- **Confirmation** (the strengthening of each Christian by the Holy Spirit)
- **Ordination** (the making of the hierarchy of bishops, priests and deacons, empowering them to administer valid sacraments)
- **Reconciliation** (confession of all serious sins to a priest, followed by an act of penance)
- **Marriage**
- **The anointing of the sick** (usually as part of the last rites)

Meanwhile, Christians are also supported from above by the heavenly hierarchies: the archangels and angels, and the saints in glory. Catholics ask for the prayers of the Blessed Virgin Mary, queen of heaven, and all the other saints, whose journey is complete and who are in the presence of God. And they pray for the souls who are still travelling upwards through purgatory.

This Catholic vision of salvation partly comes very directly from the Bible, including the main theme of reconciliation with God.[37] But the Scriptures do not mention features such as purgatory, the list of seven sacraments, or the role of Mary and the saints. And the New Testament's hope of eternal life is focussed on the arrival of the Kingdom of God on earth and the bodily resurrection of the dead on earth, rather than the journey of the soul upwards to a spiritual heaven.[38] A large part of the vision of a spiritual ascent is shaped by Greek philosophy. Ancient Greek thought dominated western scholarship from the classical world to the Middle Ages, and became a key resource and dialogue partner for theologians. The view of a higher realm of disembodied souls comes especially from Plato (c. 428-348 BC), while the theme of a process of ascent through a hierarchical cosmos derives especially from the work of the Neoplatonist philosopher Plotinus (c. 204-270 AD).

---

37   See for example 2 Corinthians 5

38   I discuss this in more detail in Chapter Seven of *The Theology of Everything*

To its supporters, this is an inspiring, optimistic and hopeful vision, giving meaning to our lives and to the ways we learn and grow, offering real change and an amazing future. They may recognise that some of its aspects go beyond the most obvious meaning of the Bible, but see this development as a divine revelation received by the Church.

However, to its critics, the Catholic vision of salvation is a serious departure from the true Gospel of Jesus Christ. It relies far too much on pagan philosophy and far too little on the true revelation found in the Bible. It makes too much of a division between soul and body. Above all, it places too much emphasis on human effort. It makes salvation seem like an epic mountaineering quest which is too dependent on our own heroic endeavours, rather than depending on the death and resurrection of Jesus. Traditional Catholicism has often been seen as fearful and obsessed with guilt, sometimes inspiring deep despair rather than hope. The most famous example of this kind of negative experience helped to start the Reformation, bringing in a very different vision of salvation.

PROTESTANTISM: JUSTIFICATION BY FAITH

Martin Luther[39] wrote this about his anxious experiences as a Catholic monk:

> The more someone tries to bring peace to his conscience
> through his own righteousness, the more disquieted he makes
> it. When I was a monk, I made a great effort to live according
> to the requirements of the monastic rule. I made a practice
> of confessing and reciting all my sins, but always with prior
> contrition; I went to confession frequently, and I performed
> the assigned penances faithfully. Nevertheless, my conscience
> could never achieve certainty but was always in doubt and said:
> 'You have not done this correctly. You were not contrite enough.
> You omitted this in your confession.' Therefore the longer I
> tried to heal my uncertain, weak and troubled conscience with

39   See p. 56

human traditions, the more uncertain, weak, and troubled I continually made it.[40]

Luther felt under enormous pressure to discipline himself, to improve himself, to carry out complex ceremonies and rituals, and to make sure he accounted for every slip up when he confessed his sins to a priest. He was not well-suited to a life of monastic celibacy, and he quickly found a former nun to marry when the Reformation began. His deep anxieties and over-scrupulous conscience also seem to have exacerbated some kind of irritable bowel syndrome.

People often turn to religion for a sense of comfort, reassurance and spiritual calm, but the Catholic Christianity of his day provided the opposite for Luther. However, as a lecturer at the University of Wittenberg, he taught courses on biblical texts, and it was in studying the Bible closely that he found the insights that led to the Reformation.

In the New Testament letters of St Paul to the Romans and Galatians, Luther saw the theme of justification by faith.[41] Paul was arguing that it was not obedience to the Jewish Law which brings salvation, but a life of faith in Jesus Christ. For Luther, that suggested that Christianity was fundamentally about trusting in what Jesus has already done for us through his death and resurrection, rather than having a hectic agenda of things that we need to do in order to improve ourselves. To be justified, meaning to be accepted by God as being in a relationship with him, had nothing to do with our own merits or achievements, but was all about God's love and mercy.

In the theology which Luther and other Reformers developed, salvation was no longer primarily about an actual change in human beings. Above all, it was about total forgiveness. We are all utterly guilty before God, but our Lord chooses to be merciful. He chooses to treat us as if we have all the righteousness shown by Christ on our behalf, even though we do not. We can 'sin boldly' as Luther said, knowing that we are simultaneously both deeply sinful in ourselves and yet are treated by God as if we had the goodness of Jesus himself.

40   From Luther's Lectures on Galatians (1535), commenting here on Galatians 5.3, in the translation by Jaroslav Pelikan (1964) *Luther's Works, Volume 27*
41   e.g. Romans 3.19-31, Galatians 2.15-16

This view of justification by faith alone allows no decisive role for human works. Like the thief dying on the cross next to Jesus who asks to be remembered by him,[42] we are freely offered a place in paradise without needing to do anything to deserve it. Such a great gift should cause a sense of gratitude which will then inspire us to do good things, and so we will there experience the transforming process of sanctification (being made more like Jesus) which is carried out by the Holy Spirit. But any later sanctification has no part in the real heart of salvation, which is primarily about being forgiven rather than about being changed. In the Protestant understanding of salvation, all those who are justified by faith are able to pass directly to heaven when they die. The Reformers rejected the belief in a long ascent through purgatory, which they could not find mentioned in the Bible.

Luther thought that, unless God helps us, we are either doomed to despair by our failure to live up to the impossible demands of God's law, or we are seduced by the delusion that our outward displays of religiosity are actually doing us some good. Strict rules and elaborate systems of church ceremonies all point to the problem of our human condition, rather than solving it. True salvation comes 'by grace alone' when we have realised the total futility of our own efforts. It is a free gift given through the abundant generosity and love of God, something that we do not remotely deserve.

This contrast in perspective about faith and works is central to the parting of ways between Protestants and Catholics in the 16th century. Catholics could not imagine salvation without our active participation and real transformation all the way through; Protestants insisted that any good works we did would only be a subsequent response of gratitude to the free gift of forgiveness received through faith. Catholics thought that salvation was all about being prepared gradually for heaven; Protestants thought that we could go straight into the presence of God as forgiven sinners. Protestantism is a bottom-up approach in that the decisive fact is the faith of the ordinary individual, not the complex Church traditions, hierarchies and rituals which are handed down to sustain that faith.

42   Luke 23.39-43

It is a difference which is still very apparent among today's churches. Evangelical churches place a huge emphasis on conversion, spreading the message that we all deserve God's punishment but can be forgiven freely if we have faith in Jesus. Evangelicals then expect the Christian life after conversion to consist primarily of spreading this message to others, seeking new converts. Evangelical Christianity often says very little about the Christian life as a journey of spiritual growth, beyond the task of understanding the Bible and explaining the Gospel to others. Many people who come to faith through Evangelicalism therefore find that they need to look elsewhere for help and guidance in deepening their life of prayer and growing closer to God. They follow a well-trodden route heading in a higher-church direction. Meanwhile, moving in the other direction are those who have found the complexities of high-church life dull or intimidating, and are drawn to a low-church approach which seems much more straightforward and vibrant.

In my experience, it has been very valuable to be able to explore both perspectives. I am one of those who has found the Evangelical approach on its own to be highly incomplete. I think that the formation of human personality and character in this life is deeply significant, especially the possibility of growing in virtue and closeness to God.[43] We are aware that life is meaningful when we build community and civilisation, when we care for each other and when we develop our talents and use them for the common good. That sense of joining in with the creative purposes of God and drawing closer to him seems to me to be an essential part of Christianity, not something secondary. Most significantly, it is strongly connected to the teachings of Jesus.

Luther believed that justification by faith is the central theme of the New Testament and the lens through which to see the rest of it. But this is a very selective reading of the Bible, driven strongly by his own personal crisis and the challenges of his own time. Although it does connect with some verses from Paul's letters, it is much less biblical than Protestants have usually assumed. In the Gospels, Jesus does not walk around Galilee explaining 'justification by faith alone' to people. In fact, he never mentions it. Instead, he proclaims the arrival

43   I explore this theme in Chapter 5 of *The Theology of Everything*

of the Kingdom of God, the reign of God on earth, and tells people to repent as well as telling them to believe. He spends much of his time on moral teaching which is inspiring and demanding, addressing both people's inner thoughts and their outward actions.[44] At no point does he say, 'You will never be able to do this, but if you have faith in me and my crucifixion then you can be forgiven.' Instead, he tells them to be perfect.[45] Nor does Paul or any other New Testament author ever say that 'justification by faith alone' is the Gospel. In fact, Paul declares that this is his Gospel: 'Remember Jesus Christ, raised from the dead, a descendent of David,'[46] a proclamation of the authority of Jesus. And in judgement, God always looks for faith that is shown in actions.[47] Finally, the Letter of James (which Luther suspected had been included in the New Testament by mistake) insists that 'faith without works is dead.'[48]

In the Bible, faith and works are always interconnected. The Reformation invention of 'justification by faith *alone*' as the heart of a new theology is an understandable reaction to medieval Catholicism's excessive focus on human efforts and rituals. But these are two sides of an unhelpful polarisation which wrongly prises apart faith and works. The new Protestant tradition is an overreaction, and it fails to meet its own criterion of being clearly grounded in the message of the whole of the Bible.

From my central perspective, faith and works seem to belong together, just as salvation involves both forgiveness and transformation by the grace of God. Though I am a Protestant, I have a lot of sympathy with the Catholic perspective, finding it very helpful that the Church offers us a treasury of practical advice, spiritual wisdom and good habits of prayer which support us along our journey. But I do think that some kind of Reformation was necessary. High-church Christianity can accumulate complexities that get in the way of a more straightforward message of forgiveness, and a thorough pruning of them from time to time by comparing them with the original message of Jesus is essential.

44 Such as the Sermon on the Mount, Matthew 5-7
45 Matthew 5.48
46 2 Timothy 2.8
47 e.g. Matthew 12.33-37, Revelation 20.11-15
48 James 2.14-26

In particular, the top-down approach always brings the temptation to exaggerate the status and powers of the clergy, which can reach the point where it starts to oppress people rather than helping them.[49]

I think my viewpoint here is probably shared by many Catholics and Protestants, and not just by some people in the middle of the Church of England. Many Protestants long for practical help with ongoing spiritual growth which goes beyond an Evangelical emphasis on conversion. And probably most of today's Catholics are content to ignore their Church's traditional claim that damnation looms if they do not confess their sins to priests. With friends on both sides in mind, I will now take a more detailed look at Catholic and Protestant understandings of the sacramental life of the Church.

SACRAMENTS

Sacraments, in a description deriving from the writings of St Augustine (354-430), are said to involve 'an outward and visible sign of an inward and spiritual grace'. The outward sign involves some kind of physical action, like pouring water on someone or immersing them in it, or breaking and sharing bread, or praying for people while laying hands on their head. There is also some kind of inward grace associated with that, some kind of work of God which is linked with the sign. Protestants and Catholics focus on different aspects of that outward and inward event.

The low-church view emphasises the inward and spiritual grace, and says that the key thing is always the individual's faith. Christianity is about justification by faith, and a sacrament is a way of proclaiming and deepening that faith. So sacraments are seen in terms of how they express and celebrate faith, giving us a physical means of pondering what God has done for us, and helping to nurture that faith. The outward sign is an expression of the inward and invisible grace.

Meanwhile, the high-church view is that the sacraments do not just symbolise God's grace, but that they actually deliver it from above, through the Church and its hierarchy of clergy. The outward sign

---

49   Some of Jesus' harshest words concern that problem – see Matthew 23

causes the inward and invisible grace. This happens because God in his great love and generosity has chosen to connect with us through sacraments, making his grace available to us in physical, tangible, objective forms, within the community of his Church. He chooses to engage our attention through material things that we can experience with our senses, rather than depending on our own ability to focus our own thoughts. Faith still matters, but part of that faith is the recognition that God is graciously making himself available to us through the sacraments.

Low-church people often think that the high-church view of sacraments sounds rather superstitious, and makes the Church look as if it is run by wizards wielding magical artefacts and chanting ancient spells. But high-church people think that sacraments are part of God's generosity, connecting with us in ways which we can touch and feel. For high-church people, this is exactly the sort of thing that you would expect following an incarnation. God who was willing for shepherds to meet him as a baby in a manger is now willing for us to meet him in bread and wine.

The Reformers decided very clearly that there are only two sacraments, since Jesus commanded baptism and the Eucharist in the Gospels and then did not mention any others. Protestants tend to be wary of any other avenues for turning Christianity into a ritualistic religion. However, there many other ceremonial practices which the Church had begun to develop in its early centuries, some of which are connected to actions described in the New Testament, and five of these are on the longer Catholic list of the seven sacraments.

There could have been even more than seven on the list. St Augustine referred to various actions as sacraments, including the giving of salt to those who were studying the Christian faith in preparation for baptism. Many ceremonies have from time to time been seen as sacramental. But tidy-minded medieval theologians liked to think that the cosmos was divinely structured around lists of seven. They thought that there were seven planets, seven virtues (with the corresponding seven deadly sins), seven archangels, seven gifts of the Holy Spirit, and that everything had been set up that way in the seven days of creation.[50] Perhaps inevitably, 12th-century Catholics also settled on the idea that there were seven sacraments. However, I find their list arbitrary, unconvincing and therefore rather self-defeating. One or two of the seven seem especially unlikely to me, and it is not clear to me why they should have been chosen instead of other ceremonies like the consecration of churches, monastic vows or the imposition of ashes at the start of Lent. Nor do some of the sacraments seem very different in character to me from a much larger list of Catholic spiritual practices, including pilgrimages to sacred places, the veneration of the bones of the saints, practical aids to prayer such as rosary beads, disciplines such as fasting, and the full dramatic celebration of the annual cycle of church festivals. However, it is an interesting list, which reveals much about the differences between Protestantism and Catholicism. I will begin with the two sacraments which are accepted by both groups and which are extremely important in the life of nearly all churches.[51]

BAPTISM

Baptism is clearly commanded in the New Testament, and is referred to in several very significant passages. The best example is the ending of Matthew's Gospel, where Jesus says to the disciples:

> All authority in heaven and on earth has been given to me. Go therefore and make disciples of all nations, baptizing them in the name of the Father and of the Son and of the Holy Spirit, and teaching them to obey everything that I have commanded you. And remember, I am with you always, to the end of the age.[52]

However, baptism had not begun with Jesus. Before Christ's ministry, John the Baptist had been baptising people in the River Jordan, immersing them under the water. It was then a sign of repentance, a way of getting ready for the coming of the Messiah. This was a symbol

50   Since I find myself irresistibly drawn to the writing of books containing seven chapters, I should probably not be too critical of this instinct.

51   The Salvation Army and the Quakers are the best known rare exceptions, emphasising the work of the Holy Spirit in a way that makes outward signs unnecessary

52   Matthew 28.18-19

that they already understood, because ritual washing before going to the Temple had long been part of Jewish practice. The original meaning of baptism therefore was repentance and the washing away of sin, but for Christians it acquired an additional symbolic status, linked to Jesus' death and resurrection.

St Paul wrote that we are baptised into the death of Christ so that we might experience new life, just as he was raised from the dead.[53] Baptism therefore means identifying ourselves with the death and resurrection of Christ. Being plunged under the water of a river is like dying and going down into the grave with Christ, and coming up afterwards is like a resurrection. Baptism means having our old sinful self put to death and buried, so that we can then be newly alive with Christ.

The New Testament presents baptism in this way as a normal part of what happens when people become Christians. Early in the Acts of the Apostles, there is an account of 3000 people being baptised on the Day of Pentecost after hearing the preaching of Peter. He says that those who repent and are baptised will receive forgiveness of sins and the gift of the Holy Spirit[54] (a subject which I shall return to in the section on Confirmation).

The obvious reading of this is to say that baptism cleanses us from our own sins. But St Augustine later emphasised that it is not just our own life which is the problem, but the human condition which we have inherited. In his understanding of the Fall, all of Adam and Eve's descendants inherit their guilt, and only the sacrament of baptism can cleanse us from this stain. This view of original sin remains an important part of the Catholic understanding of baptism.[55]

Protestants have largely moved away from Augustine's idea of washing away the guilt of Adam and Eve, but still share his emphasis on the universal sinfulness of the human race, which establishes the need for a saving faith. From a Protestant perspective, it is the faith of the person being baptised which matters, or the faith of the parents

---

53   Romans 6.3-4
54   Acts 2.38,41
55   For my criticism of St Augustine's view of the Fall, see p. 131 of *The Theology of Everything*

and godparents bringing a child for baptism. It is a step of trust and obedience, the outward sign of the beginning of the Christian life.

Catholic language tends to emphasise that God works through the water and the actions of the priest, while Protestant language tends to emphasise that God works through the faith of the individual. Low-church people might worry that the high-church perspective sounds all rather superstitious, as if Christians were talking about magic water. But high-church people think that they are asserting something about the grace of God. They are proclaiming that the grace of God is freely offered, in a way which can be made visible and obvious. They see this as something that God does objectively, which does not depend on our own ability to come up with the right subjective response. From either perspective, both groups see baptism as associated with the normal beginning of the Christian life.

But the biggest difference in today's Church regarding baptism is the attitude to the baptism of infants (popularly known as christening). Catholics, Orthodox and most Protestants are happy to baptise the children of Christian parents, assuming that they will be brought up in the faith. But the most Evangelical parts of the Church have adopted the approach which the radical Anabaptists pioneered at the Reformation: baptism must be left until people are old enough to declare for themselves that they truly have faith. This view has grown within the Evangelical movement alongside the increasing emphasis on liberty in the West, as I described in Chapter Two.

While infant baptism usually involves only pouring three small dribbles of water on the head (to minimise distress to the baby), those who reserve baptism for adults prefer to immerse them fully in a special baptistry pool. This much more dramatic method returns to something closer to the practice described in the New Testament, expressing more obviously the symbolism of dying and rising with Christ. For Evangelicals, baptism can function very dramatically as a celebration of the event of conversion which they emphasise so strongly.

Those Evangelicals who do not baptise children think that they are faithfully following the Bible. But there is a genuine difficulty over interpretation here, since the New Testament does not explicitly address the question of infant baptism. Without any clear comment from Jesus or the Apostles, we need to look back to the Old Testament to see the kinds of assumptions which the New Testament authors would have held.

The Old Testament describes how baby boys were circumcised at 8 days old, symbolising that all Jewish infants were regarded as full members of the people of God from the very beginning of their lives. There was no decision for them to make to opt in, and it still remains the case today that someone is considered to be Jewish if their mother is. The background, default biblical understanding of infants seems to be that they join in with whatever is going on with their parents. They naturally acquire the faith of their family and their community, and are members from their earliest days.

The New Testament does not discuss that assumption, and never affirms or rejects the baptism of infants. The closest it gets to it is references to the whole household of Lydia being baptised after her conversion, and the whole family of a jailer being baptised after he came to faith.[56] The text does not bother to tell us whether the youngest members of the households in question were two weeks old or 16 years old, which suggests that Luke did not see it as a significant issue. Nor does it say that there was a heated discussion in the household before everyone was persuaded of the truth of the Gospel. But the world of the New Testament included much less of an emphasis on individual freedom and choice than is expected by Evangelicals today. There was probably much more of an expectation that everyone would agree to whatever the head of the household decided.

Finally, there is no mention in the New Testament or the writings of the early Church of the custom of dedicating babies to God, which often now happens in churches which do not baptise them. Nor is there any evidence of a time in the early Church when people thought that infant baptism was invalid, or a time when that practice is recorded as beginning. The continuous tradition of the Church until the Reformation suggests support for infant baptism.

The highest-church perspective approves of infant baptism as an objective source of grace for the child, a genuine cleansing of the baby

56 Acts 16.14-15, 33

from the guilt of original sin, removing the stain of our inheritance from the rebellion of Adam and Eve. Even a light sprinkling of holy water administered in the name of the Trinity will suffice. Without this, St Augustine feared that a child who died unbaptised could at best go to limbo, not to heaven. The lowest-church perspective rejects infant baptism because it insists that the holy water achieves nothing in itself. Instead, it prefers the full immersion of genuine converts, which provides a dramatic statement of their faith and a turning point in their lives.

In my case, I am glad that my atheist parents did not have me christened as an infant. I made a decision as a young adult to become a Christian, and being plunged under the water in my baptism was a very significant milestone in my life. However, I know many people who have grown up in Christian households and who cannot remember a time when they did not have some kind of faith in Jesus Christ. To them, it feels exactly right that they were baptised as infants.

My view is that baptising the children of practising Christians is compatible with the New Testament. It is the continuous tradition of most of the Church, and it continues to be meaningful and appropriate. However, there is a dilemma in churches which baptise infants. What do we do when people who never otherwise come to church bring their children for baptism? Often this is because of a family tradition for celebrating births and naming children in this way, and sometimes it is only one enthusiastic grandparent who is demanding its continuation. What does baptism still mean if the child will not really be brought up in the faith? What do we do if the parents and godparents are making promises in the service which they will not keep?

Opinions among Church of England clergy vary. The majority will offer an unconditional welcome, while a minority (usually Evangelicals) will try very hard to get the parents to go on a course first. Either approach will sometimes succeed in giving the whole family such a positive experience of the Church that they will keep coming back. But often this does not work. A higher-church person may feel that some hidden good has been done by the power of the sacrament. A lower-church person may worry that the family has been given a taste of the outward trappings of religion without any understanding of the faith itself. I have to admit that I have felt all of those things at different times, and am left with more sympathy for the lower-church view. This is one of the tensions of living in a society which has moved away from Christian faith but still sometimes uses Church ceremonies as rites of passage.

In today's world, I think we should expect adults to form a higher proportion of those being baptised. Fewer children have churchgoing parents who give them a genuinely Christian upbringing or send them off to Sunday School. Faith is increasingly something that people come to for themselves when they are old enough to make their own decisions, and it is appropriate to celebrate that with a full immersion baptism. Warm countries can still use rivers in the oldest tradition. For those of us in cooler climates, I think that a key part of any major church refurbishment should be the installation of a baptismal pool for adults, deep enough for us to celebrate this sacrament with all of the drama and symbolism that it first held.

THE EUCHARIST

The second of the two sacraments instituted by Jesus Christ in the Gospels is the Eucharist. While baptism happens only once and marks the beginning of the Christian life, the Eucharist is the food for the journey which is received many times. It is the weekly form of Sunday worship for the majority of the world's churchgoers. The Eucharist is one of various names for the sacrament which Catholics usually call the Mass and which Protestants tend to call Holy Communion, the Lord's Supper or the Breaking of Bread.

The Eucharist involves the blessing and sharing of bread and wine, following on from the actions of Jesus at his Last Supper on the night before he was crucified. The gospels of Matthew, Mark and Luke, echoed by Paul in his First Letter to the Corinthians, together describe this Passover meal. Jesus took the bread and said, 'Take, eat; this is my body which is given for you; do this in remembrance of me.' Later, he shared the cup of wine, saying 'Drink this, all of you; this is my blood of the new covenant, which is shed for you and for many for the forgiveness of sins. Do this, as often as you drink it, in remembrance of me.'[57] Jesus built upon the Jewish symbolism of the annual Passover, which commemorates God's great act of salvation in the Old Testament, the rescue of the people of Israel from slavery in Egypt.[58] He developed it with reference to his own approaching death, the salvation described in the New Testament, declaring a new covenant between people and God. The repetition of these actions in the Eucharist became the distinctive Christian act of worship in the early Church.

Two very different perspectives on the Eucharist have been explored since its beginnings, seeing it either as a meal or as a sacrifice. When thinking of it as a meal, Christians may think of Jesus feeding and sustaining them, offering his life for them, and may find that the most appropriate setting is to gather around a wooden table. When thinking of it as a sacrifice, Christians may think of their priest offering the crucified Christ to God the Father, and may find that the most appropriate setting is for the priest and the congregation to face towards a stone altar. The two perspectives have been explored in overlapping ways, but the meal is inherently the lower-church perspective, seeming more like an ordinary thing which any group of Christians could do. Meanwhile, the sacrifice is inherently the higher-church perspective, suggesting the need for a validly-ordained priest who is empowered to stand at the altar between the people and God and to offer the sacrifice on their behalf.

Out of these two perspectives, it is the theme of a shared meal which is most directly present in the Bible. The Acts of the Apostles talks of the first Christians meeting on a Sunday to break bread together,[59] which sounds like some kind of community meal. But this was always more than a routine dinner. St Paul rebuked those who greedily gobbled up too much bread or got drunk on the wine,[60] telling them to fill up at home. It was a meal with a meaning, rather than a plentiful source of calories. St Paul also expressed the earliest suggestion that there is something miraculous that happens through the bread and the wine:

57   Matthew 26.26-27, Mark 14.22-23, Luke 22.18-20, 1 Corinthians 11.23-25
58   Exodus 12
59   Acts 20.7
60   1 Cor 11.21-22, 34

> The cup of blessing that we bless, is it not a sharing in the blood
> of Christ? The bread that we break, is it not a sharing in the
> body of Christ?[61]

A similar idea can be found in John's Gospel, which lacks any mention of bread and wine at the Last Supper but seems to refer to the Eucharist in an earlier chapter. Jesus says:

> I am the living bread that came down from heaven. Whoever
> eats of this bread will live forever… Unless you eat the flesh
> of the Son of Man and drink his blood, you have no life in you.
> Those who eat my flesh and drink my blood have eternal life,
> and I will raise them up on the last day.[62]

These passages in the New Testament suggest that the Eucharist is a meal, but it is a meal in which we are in some sense fed by Jesus' own self, sharing in his body and blood through the blessing and sharing of bread and wine.

By contrast, the Bible provides no explicit and direct connection between the Eucharist and the theme of sacrifice. However, it does use sacrificial imagery extensively in relation to Jesus and his death. Jewish priests routinely carried out animal sacrifices in the great Temple in Jerusalem in Jesus' time, as did the religions of the surrounding nations in their own shrines. However distasteful it seems to us today, the instinct to perform sacrifices was very widespread among the farming communities of the ancient world, where daily life depended on the nurture and killing of animals. The Letter to the Hebrews therefore uses imagery then very familiar when it describes Jesus as a high priest, offering his own blood in a sacrifice that can purify all people and establish a new covenant between them and God, a sacrifice which never needs to be repeated.[63]

These were familiar concepts in ancient religion, and it is not surprising that a sacrificial understanding of Jesus' death had become

---

61   1 Corinthians 10.16
62   John 6.51-54
63   Hebrews 7 to 10. For a more detailed discussion of the meaning of Jesus' death, see Chapter
     Six of *The Theology of Everything*

connected with the Eucharist by the late first century. Dating from around that time, the Didache says this about Sunday worship:

> On the Lord's own day gather together and break bread and
> give thanks, having first confessed your sins so that your
> sacrifice may be pure. But let no one who has a quarrel with
> a companion join you until they have been reconciled, so
> that your sacrifice may not be defiled. For this is the sacrifice
> concerning which the Lord said, 'In every place and time offer
> me a pure sacrifice, for I am a great king, says the Lord, and my
> name is marvellous among the nations.'[64]

That last sentence is a reference to the words of the Old Testament prophet Malachi,[65] in a passage about the corruption of the Temple priesthood. Early Christians came to believe that the Eucharist was the pure sacrifice which fulfilled Malachi's prophesy. The bread and the wine were in some sense the body and blood of Christ, and the Eucharist involved somehow making that sacrifice present and offering it to God.

In this way, Ignatius of Antioch, in his Letter to the Smyrnaeans in 108 AD, insisted that the Eucharist was 'the flesh of our Saviour Jesus Christ, which suffered for our sins, and which the Father, of His goodness, raised up again.'[66] And Justin Martyr said (c. 155 AD):

> Not as common bread and common drink do we receive
> these… we have been taught that the food which is blessed by
> the prayer of his word, and from which our blood and flesh
> by transmutation are nourished, is the flesh and blood of that
> Jesus who was made flesh.[67]

---

64   Didache, Chapter 14 - this translation from Michael W Holmes (2007) *The Apostolic Fathers* Baker Academic

65   Malachi 1.11

66   Letter of St Ignatius to the Smyrnaeans, Chapter 6 – this translation from Michael W Holmes (2007) *The Apostolic Fathers* Baker Academic

67   First Apology, Chapter LXVI – as translated in Alexander Roberts and James Donaldson, eds (1999) *Ante-Nicene Fathers: Volume 1* Hendrickson

Nevertheless, the theme of a shared meal was still dominant in Justin's writing, which includes the earliest known detailed account of Christian Sunday worship:

> On the day called Sunday, all who live in cities or in the country gather together to one place, and the memoirs of the apostles or the writings of the prophets are read, as long as time permits; then, when the reader has ceased, the president verbally instructs, and exhorts to the imitation of these good things. Then we all rise together and pray, and… when our prayer is ended, bread and wine and water are brought, and the president in like manner offers prayers and thanksgivings, according to his ability, and the people assent, saying Amen; and there is a distribution to each, and a participation of that over which thanks have been given, and to those who are absent a portion is sent by the deacons.[68]

It means a lot to me that Justin Martyr's description fits the worship we have normally on Sunday mornings in the Chapel where I lead services. The memoirs of the apostles are the writings which later became our New Testament, which we read from every week. As he says, there is a sermon which exhorts people to imitate these good things. We pray, and we give thanks over bread and wine and share it. With some variations, this has been the pattern of worship for the majority of the world's Christians throughout the last 20 centuries.

After Justin's time, the sacrificial theme was explored further and the theme of the shared meal began to recede. From the fourth century, Christians were able to build churches, and the focus of worship shifted from homes to sacred places which were increasingly grand. They believed that Christian ministry involved a priesthood which was empowered by God to offer the sacrifice of the Eucharist, a perspective which evolved as an essential part of the top-down view of the Church. Early Catholic liturgy expresses this theme powerfully, as seen here in some of the words spoken at the altar by priests using the Roman Canon, which dates from somewhere in the middle of the first millennium:

68   Chapter LXVII, as above

Therefore, O Lord,
as we celebrate the memorial of the blessed Passion,
the Resurrection from the dead,
and the glorious Ascension into heaven
of Christ, your Son, our Lord,
we, your servants and your holy people,
offer to your glorious majesty
from the gifts that you have given us,
this pure victim,
this holy victim,
this spotless victim,
the holy Bread of eternal life
and the Chalice of everlasting salvation...

In humble prayer we ask you, almighty God:
command that these gifts be borne
by the hands of your holy Angel
to your altar on high
in the sight of your divine majesty,
so that all of us, who through this participation at the altar
receive the most holy Body and Blood of your Son,
may be filled with every grace and heavenly blessing.[69]

This view of the Eucharist as a holy sacrifice offered up to God by priests was shared by eastern and western Christians in the first millennium. But some differences began to emerge. Catholics came to believe that it was central to the life of priests that they should all offer the sacrifice of the Mass every day, and began to construct churches with additional side chapels so that all the clergy in religious communities could celebrate their own daily Masses. Durham Cathedral and Fountains Abbey each have nine altars in parallel chapels for this purpose. The continual daily offering of the Eucharist on behalf of Christians on earth and in purgatory was seen as the essential heart of the ministry of priests and of the life of the Church, overshadowing the idea of a shared meal.

---

69   This appears as Eucharistic Prayer I in the Ordinary Form of the Roman Rite Mass, as printed in *The CTS New Sunday Missal* in 2011 by the Catholic Truth Society

Orthodox thinkers were more content to leave the Eucharist as a glorious and holy mystery, while western scholarship during the Middle Ages began to take a rigorously analytical approach to understanding it. The most notable figure in the project was the greatest of all medieval Catholic theologians, St Thomas Aquinas (1225-1274). Through his work, Catholics came to define the presence of Christ in the Eucharist as *transubstantiation*. Aquinas was using the ancient philosophy of Aristotle (384–322 BC), which had recently been rediscovered and was the best available science at the time. Aristotelian philosophy routinely makes a distinction between the outward form of something and its inward substance. He concluded that the outward form of the bread and the wine remained the same, but that the inward substance changed into the body and blood of Christ. Catholics understand that change of substance to happen at the exact moments when the priest repeats the words spoken by Christ at the last supper: 'This is my body... This is my blood.' Often, bells are rung at those two points in the Mass.

This very precise and philosophical analysis of the Eucharist was associated with two sets of practical consequences which arose among Catholics but not among the Orthodox, and which were subsequently rejected by Protestants. Firstly, Aquinas taught that the whole and entire presence of Christ was found in any crumb of consecrated bread or drop of consecrated wine. Receiving half a wafer did not mean only half receiving Christ. Medieval ceremonial paid great attention to keeping hold of crumbs and carefully drinking up every drop of wine, placing communion wafers directly on to the tongues of recipients. The messy task of serving alcohol to the laity, fraught with the risk of spilling the precious blood, ceased on the grounds that they would have received Christ entirely from the bread. Wine therefore became an almost superfluous part of the ceremony in the west, only consumed by the priests. At the same time, receiving the actual body of Christ became such an awesome and terrifying prospect for lay-people that they might only take communion a few times each year, despite attending Mass each week. The real point of the Eucharist now seemed to be to watch the offering of the sacrifice to God, while the idea of a shared meal was further pushed into the background.

Secondly, the intense focus on the bread and wine as genuinely divine in themselves led to new forms of Catholic worship which were separate from the context of the Eucharist. Consecrated wafers began to be put aside after a Mass not just to be taken to be eaten by the sick and the housebound (as Justin Martyr described in the second century), but also to be displayed on other occasions as objects of worship. The separate service of Benediction was devised, in which a priest holds up the eucharistic bread in an elaborate golden stand, using it to bless the congregation. And the lavish customs of the annual feast of Corpus Christi developed, in which a consecrated communion wafer is carried in a great outdoor procession, held aloft under a splendid canopy, often with girls preparing the way by throwing flowers on the road ahead.

I find it very interesting that the Eucharist begins as a set of actions ('do this', 'take and eat this,' 'drink this, all of you'), which are then processed twelve centuries later through a philosophical system, which then outputs a greatly modified set of actions. Jesus said that all should drink the wine, but Catholic philosophy tells us that the wine adds nothing to the bread and can be withheld from the laity, cutting out half of the people's participation. While Jesus only mentions the bread in direct connection with the actions of taking, blessing, breaking and eating, Catholic philosophy tells us that we can worship the bread as a way of worshipping Jesus, leading to a whole set of very different actions.

These medieval developments were an obvious target for the scepticism of the Reformers in the 16th century, when people began to compare such elaborate customs with the origins of the Eucharist described in the New Testament. Protestants rebelled to varying degrees against the Catholic view of the Eucharist, seeing Catholic ceremonial complexities as human inventions rather than divine gifts. They thought that Christianity was not about benefitting from sacrifices offered by priests, or any kind of obedience to rituals, but was about being justified by faith. They thought that the Catholic reverence towards the consecrated bread was idolatrous. And they thought that the Eucharist found its meaning in the ways that it proclaimed and nurtured faith in Jesus and in his one complete sacrifice on the cross.

Protestants therefore simplified or abandoned the elaborate liturgies of the Catholic Mass. They removed the theme of the sacrifice of Christ's body and blood offered by priests, sometimes talking instead of a sacrifice of praise given by the congregation, and greatly reemphasised the theme of the shared meal. Often they rearranged church buildings so that the architectural focus was now on a pulpit for the preaching of sermons, rather than on an altar. The furnishings used for communion became something more like a simple dining table and less like an elaborately decorated place of sacrifice. One thing was added: obedience to Jesus' command that all should share in in the wine.

Protestants rejected the Catholic philosophy of transubstantiation, but struggled to agree on a well-defined alternative. Lutherans spoke of a 'sacramental union', in which the body and blood of Christ are united with the bread and the wine and are received by those eating and drinking. But there was a strong pull towards the much simpler definition known as memorialism: the bread and wine remain entirely unchanged, and function as symbols which help the worshipper to remember Jesus and his death. In this view, it is the faith and experience of the Christians receiving the sacrament which matters, not the bread and wine themselves.

However, it seemed to many that such drastic reforms involved throwing too much away. As I described earlier, there was enough in the New Testament to suggest that the bread and the wine were much more than mere symbols. And the beauty and reverence of the Catholic liturgy still had its admirers among Protestants. In the Church of England, some of the content of the Catholic Mass was translated and adapted within a new English service of Holy Communion, which now insisted that Christ's one perfect and sufficient sacrifice for the sins of the whole world was being remembered, rather than being made present and offered again. Yet there was enough of the traditional liturgy to preserve a sense of wonder and mystery. The practice of kneeling in front of the communion table to take communion was continued, but now with the chalice of wine being placed into the hands of the laity rather than kept only for the priest.

In this view, the Eucharist was definitely a meal at a table and not a sacrifice at an altar, but some ambiguity remained over the manner in which Christ was encountered through that meal. In the first *Book of Common Prayer* of 1549, the liturgy still conveyed a more Catholic sense that the bread and wine were to be identified as the body and blood of Christ, having a direct effect on our bodies as well as our souls. The priest would use these words when distributing the bread and wine:

> The Body of our Lord Jesus Christ, which was given for thee, preserve thy body and soul unto everlasting life.

> The Blood of our Lord Jesus Christ, which was shed for thee, preserve thy body and soul unto everlasting life.

In 1552, things had moved in a much more Protestant direction, and the words were completely changed to emphasise things happening within the inner life of the recipients: remembering, giving thanks, believing.

> Take and eat this in remembrance that Christ died for thee, and feed on him in thy heart by faith with thanksgiving.

> Drink this in remembrance that Christ's Blood was shed for thee, and be thankful.

England became Catholic again in 1553 and then returned to Protestantism in 1559, after which Queen Elizabeth I made a careful attempt to unite all of the Christians of her realm. She combined both sets of words, so that the liturgy allowed both perspectives, pointing to an encounter with Christ that does not need a perfect definition. Today's Church of England liturgies join them all together as an invitation to the congregation:

> Draw near with faith.
> Receive the body of our Lord Jesus Christ
> which he gave for you,
> and his blood which he shed for you.

Eat and drink
in remembrance that he died for you,
and feed on him in your hearts
by faith with thanksgiving.[70]

To me, the Protestant liturgy of the *Book of Common Prayer* is a work of genius, for which I am very grateful. It removes the excesses and errors of medieval Catholicism and recovers the perspective of the New Testament, without overreacting in the manner of most Protestants. It achieves an elegant balance, presenting a very reverent and beautiful way of celebrating the Eucharist which illuminates the New Testament sense of sharing in the body and blood of Christ.

In the clash between a Catholic belief in transubstantiation and the Protestant overreaction of memorialism, both sides seem to me to have over-analysed things in a way which is alien to the approach found in the Bible. Both sides want to pull the Eucharist apart to find some underlying mechanism, whether in the substance of the bread or the souls of the worshipper.

I do not like the medieval Catholic idea that you can dismantle the whole event of the Eucharist and locate the miracle in a few of the words and in some of the matter. I do not believe in transubstantiation because I do not believe in the underlying Aristotelian philosophy. I am uncomfortable about transubstantiation's logical consequences, such as removing the consecrated bread from the context of the Eucharist and presenting it as an object of adoration. On the other hand, neither do I think that you can dismantle the whole event of the Eucharist and locate the divine action entirely in what happens inside the minds and hearts of the worshippers. I think it is the drama of the Eucharist as a whole which is important.

My perspective from the middle ground is therefore that I would rather talk about the Eucharist as an event. Where high-church people focus on 'This is my body', and low-church people on 'remembrance of me' in Jesus' words, I think that rather more emphasis is needed on his command to 'do this'. The Eucharist is the continuation of a dramatic

---

70   This appeared in *The Alternative Service Book* (1980) and continues in the current *Common Worship* (2000)

tradition which joins us to the events of the crucifixion and resurrection, in ways which connect with our senses, souls and bodies and which bind us together as a community.

So I will return to those words of St Paul, the first known writer on the Eucharist:

> The cup of blessing that we bless, is it not a sharing in the blood of Christ? The bread that we break, is it not a sharing in the body of Christ? Because there is one bread, we who are many are one body, for we all partake of the one bread.[71]

It is from that word *sharing* that we get the term *communion*. To say that the cup is a *sharing* in the blood of Christ seems to me to be saying that it is a lot more than a disposable dramatic prop, but still falls short of saying that the wine physically changes to become the blood of Christ. Paul puts the emphasis on the verbs: blessing, breaking, sharing, partaking, rather than on an analysis of the matter. It is those actions which seem to me to significant, together with the liturgy which they shape.

It seems to me that there is something real, powerful, awesome, wondrous and objective about what God does through the bread and wine of the Eucharist. But I also think that our response of faith is very important. This is a relationship, in which both sides matter. I feel that there is a physical encounter with Jesus Christ in the Eucharist which is the closest I get to being able to touch God. I believe that Jesus took on human flesh so that people really could meet him 2000 years ago, using their human senses to connect with the reality of God, and that God continues to make himself knowable to our senses in and through the Eucharist. God chooses to use physical matter to relate to me, because I am a physical creature with senses of sight, smell, touch, taste and hearing. The Eucharist engages all those senses very profoundly, along with my mind and my soul and my experience of relating to the people around me.

Taking that approach, I would agree with the Catholic view that the Eucharist is the Church's main act of worship, normally to be celebrated

---

71   1 Corinthians 10.16-17

by Christians on all Sundays and major festivals. At the same time, I would agree with the Protestant emphasis that the Eucharist is primarily to be understood as a sacred meal given to us, rather than as a way of offering the sacrifice of Christ to the Father.

I think that there are also things to learn from high and low celebrations of the Eucharist. Just as full immersion baptisms are to be encouraged, appreciating their drama and symbolism to the full, I think that the drama and symbolism of the Eucharist should also be made as obvious as possible, avoiding any cautious minimalism. Where possible, the bread should all begin in one piece before being broken and shared, emphasising that we are sharing together in the body of Christ, united in him. Individual wafers may still be needed for very large congregations, but seem unfortunate to me unless they are absolutely necessary. For the same reasons, there should if possible be one cup which all drink from. When fortified wine is used in a silver chalice, wiped between each person, this is perfectly safe. And the wine should be a strong red wine, deep in colour to symbolise blood, and rich in flavour. It should be real wine containing very noticeable alcohol (aside from in any special provision being made for alcoholics).

Through the quirks of history, high-church people tend to have one cup of wine and many wafers, while low-church people may have one bread roll and many cups of grape juice. I would prefer to draw on the best of both perspectives.

I must bring my history of Catholicism up to date by mentioning that Catholic theology has itself moved somewhat in the direction of that middle ground over the last 50 years. There was a very fruitful convergence of Catholic and Protestant liturgical scholarship in the 20th century. The 1970 revision of the Mass, following the Second Vatican Council, introduced services in modern languages, reduced the emphasis on sacrifice, restored the possibility of lay people receiving the wine on some occasions, and moved church altars away from the east wall. The priest could now face the congregation across the altar, reintroducing a sense that this was a meal shared around a table. However, the replacement of the traditional Latin Mass by something more friendly and accessible has been a matter of great controversy among Catholics, a theme which I will return to in the next chapter.

The most recent demonstration of different views of the Eucharist occurred during the COVID-19 pandemic lockdowns of 2020, when it was interesting to see how the themes of sacrifice and meal were expressed instinctively in the services offered online by different kinds of church. Those for whom the sacrificial theme still resonates strongly often took great comfort from the online streaming of services where a solitary priest celebrated the Eucharist at the altar in an otherwise empty building. They could see that the sacrifice was still being offered in the holy place on their behalf, and could watch it with devotion in the way that they would normally watch from their pew. But those for whom the theme of a shared meal is dominant were likely to find such lonely spectacles rather baffling. Lower churches often preferred more interactive services on Zoom, enabling different people to lead different parts of the service. And, if there was communion, they sometimes encouraged people at home to participate with their own supplies of bread and wine. Higher church people shuddered at this blurring of sacred boundaries: was the domestic bread and wine truly conse-crated at a distance and, if so, was Jesus then being treated with all due reverence?

CONFIRMATION

I move on now to the five ceremonies regarded by Catholics and Ortho-dox as sacraments, but not by Protestants, beginning with Confirmation. This can trace its beginnings to the New Testament, although not to anything commanded by Jesus. The Acts of the Apostles describes the baptism of new Christians, and also mentions a practice where the apostles placed their hands on them and prayed for them to receive the Holy Spirit.[72]

The practice is not given a name and is simply narrated as some-thing that happened on some occasions. In Acts, it is associated with very obvious signs of the workings of the Holy Spirit, such as people

---

72   Acts 8.14-17 and Acts 19.1-7

speaking in tongues and prophesying. Elsewhere, St Paul writes to Timothy telling him to 'rekindle the gift of God that is within you through the laying on of my hands.'[73]

Confirmation therefore developed as a ceremony in which a bishop places hands on someone's head and prays for them to be *confirmed*, which means *strengthened*, by the Holy Spirit. This has become a normal part of Christian initiation for Catholics, Orthodox, Anglicans and some other Protestants.

The outward sign in confirmation is the laying on of hands, and often also an anointing with oil as a symbol of the Holy Spirit. Confirmation was originally closely connected with baptism, as it still is in Orthodoxy. The Orthodox refer to it as *chrismation*, which is an anointing carried out during the baptism service itself.

However, in the western churches, a separation arose between baptism and the subsequent prayers for the receiving of the Holy Spirit. The anointing with oil and the laying on of hands became something which was only done by bishops when they visited, and therefore became separate from baptism, which was done by priests. A western tradition of confirmation being associated with the teenage years then gradually developed. Confirmation also therefore acquired a sense that this was an opportunity for young people to be given a course of instruction about Christianity, and to have an opportunity to confirm their faith for themselves, which is where most people wrongly assume the name comes from. Nevertheless, the primary meaning of confirmation remains the prayer for the candidates to be strengthened by the Holy Spirit, so that they may serve God in the church and the world as people with a mature faith.

In my experience in the Church of England, confirmation is often a very meaningful milestone in someone's journey of faith and their involvement in the Church. The visit of a bishop to lead the service is an excellent way of symbolising that those who are baptised and confirmed have a place in the global Church as well as in the local congregation.

---

73   2 Timothy 1:6-7

ORDINATION

There are similarities between Confirmation and Ordination, which have the same basic action. The Acts of the Apostles describes the apostles appointing seven deacons by praying for them and laying hands on them.[74] In the early Church, this became the way in which bishops ordained bishops, priests and deacons, within the threefold system which I have fully discussed in Chapter Two. For Catholics, a valid ordination within the apostolic succession is the key to those other sacraments which require a priest or bishop to officiate.

After Confirmation and Ordination, the remaining three Catholic sacraments start to look much less convincing to me.

EXTREME UNCTION

The Letter of James describes the elders of the church praying for the sick and anointing them with oil as a way of seeking healing.[75] This is seen as the biblical basis for the sacrament called extreme unction, which was supposed to be about praying for the recovery of someone who was ill. But it has evolved instead to become part of the last rites, reversing its meaning. It is something which is only normally done when someone is confidently expected to die, rather than being something which is expected to bring healing.

The anointing of the terminally ill seems to me to have no convincing roots in the New Testament. I think that Catholics have sometimes been unnecessarily anxious about the spiritual state of those who are dying, worrying too much about the need for dying in a state of grace. The most diligent Catholic priests have taken great care to make sure that dying people have confessed all of their sins, taken communion and been anointed with oil. Spending time with the dying and saying familiar prayers with them is a loving and supportive thing to do, but I am wary of anything that over-emphasises human responsibility at a time of great frailty. Any of us may end up in a deeply confused state as death approaches, perhaps suffering from dementia, perhaps

74   Acts 6.1-6
75   James 5.14

regressing to instinctive forms of behaviour which do not reflect well on us. I trust that God will gather up our true selves, looking at the totality of the decisions we have made when in our right minds, rather than relying on the rituals of the final moments of life.

Meanwhile, the practice of anointing the sick with oil in the hope that they may actually be healed has become more popular again in some circles, especially among Charismatics, following that passage from James. They are much closer to the original meaning of that text, but the new wave of low-church enthusiasts for anointing would not use the term sacrament to describe it.

CONFESSION

The same passage in James also tells Christians to confess their sins to each other.[76] This is seen as the biblical basis for the sacrament called penance, or reconciliation, which involves individuals confessing their sins to a priest. But James does not make any mention of a special role for church leaders in the practice of people owing up to their misdeeds. Nevertheless, by the Middle Ages, confession to a priest was seen as the essential way in which people received God's forgiveness for their sins. Sins labelled as 'mortal sins', a long list which included failing to go to church every Sunday, were understood as a full and deliberate rejection of God, terminating a person's eternal salvation. Those who had committed such sins would be on their way to hell, until making a full confession of their wrongdoing to a priest and doing a work of penance allotted by him. The penance would include prayers, and perhaps actions such as fasting or giving money to the poor or to the Church.

Here I think we move deeper into unconvincing territory, and into something potentially sinister. I am very glad that my life as a Christian minister does not involve having to spend hours each week sitting in a cubicle listening to nervous people apologising for their lustful thoughts. People do come and sit in an armchair in my study to talk about situations in life which they find challenging, including dilemmas, destructive habits, and struggles in their prayer life. I listen a lot

76   James 5.16

and advise a little, and keep them in my prayers. This fits the pattern described in the *Book of Common Prayer*, which suggests that those who cannot quiet their own consciences should seek the counsel of a minister of God's word.[77] Informally, I communicate a sense that they are understood and forgiven, and sometimes it is clear that my involvement has helped to get someone out of a mess which they could not have climbed out of on their own. But I see this as pastoral support for those in particular need, rather than as something essential for all people in every season of their lives. Nor do I think it is a uniquely priestly role, as there are many wise lay people who exercise the same kind of ministry among their friends from time to time.

Recent decades have also seen a widening interest in the practice of *spiritual direction*, an arrangement where one person acts as a guide and helper to another in their life of prayer and Christian service, perhaps agreeing to meet monthly or a few times a year. This was originally a high-church practice, usually carried out by priests who could also hear confessions. But it is now often found among lower churches as well, and spiritual directors are often lay people, informally supporting others who are exploring their sense of vocation and spirituality.

In the confession of sins, the Church of England is confident that people will find God's forgiveness through their own private prayers and through the prayers of penitence which we say together at the start of services. The idea that everyone has to admit all of their embarrassing failures to the clergy in order to be forgiven by God is something that I find very intrusive. Protestants, following Luther, rejected it five centuries ago. And the majority of today's Catholics seem to agree with me, as they are going to confession very rarely. The Catholic teaching remains officially unchangeable, but confession has become perhaps an annual event for the most devout, rather than a frequent practice for everyone.

---

77   From the first exhortation in the Communion service

MARRIAGE

Finally, there is marriage. Putting this in the same category as baptism and the Eucharist seems to me to be highly unconvincing. Marriage is certainly mentioned in the New Testament, including an account of Jesus going to the wedding in Cana. But there is nothing at all in the Bible to suggest that marriages are formed through religious ceremonies. The only weddings mentioned in the Bible seem to consist of large amounts of eating[78] or drinking.[79] Many centuries went past before churches started seeing religious wedding ceremonies as being a normal part of what they did. That surprises most people today, who tend to think that weddings are second only to carol services on the list of the principal activities of churches. But church weddings have nothing at all to do with the teachings of Jesus or the practices of the early Church. Jesus himself advocated singleness for those who could accept it, as did St Paul.[80]

All of the other Catholic sacraments have some special connection with the salvation brought by Jesus Christ. But marriage is something found throughout all cultures and throughout history. As the Church of England's services say, it is a 'gift of God in creation'. Though given by God, it is no more specifically Christian than breathing. It is simply something that people do in all times and places, with or without the help of Christian clergy. The practice of regulating marriage by state-approved churches which issue official government certificates is a phenomenon of the last few centuries.

Catholics came to understand marriage as one of the seven sacraments in the 12th century, thereby establishing what seems to me to be a very confusing situation. The Roman Catholic Church first recognised that the ministers of the sacrament of marriage were the couple themselves, but since 1563 has insisted that Catholic marriages must take place in a church ceremony led by a Catholic priest. This leads to an odd set of rules in which Catholics regard marriages between non-Catholics as being real and indissoluble marriages, but say that only marriages

78   Genesis 29.22
79   John 2.1-11
80   Matthew 19.12, 1 Corinthians 7.8

in a Catholic church are in some way a sacrament. Catholic theology is especially muddled at this point, and I have never been able to find a convincing account of what the real difference between a sacramental wedding and any other wedding is. This muddle has also made it harder to talk clearly about same-sex marriage, which I will return to in Chapter Six.

Catholic theology has also arrived at an unconvincing conclusion with regard to divorce. The Old Testament law permits divorce, so a man could dismiss a wife simply by writing a declaration and sending her away with it.[81] This meant that a man who casually gave up on a marriage could still regard himself as a completely moral, law-abiding person. In the New Testament, Jesus introduces a new perspective, saying that this law is a concession to people's hard-heartedness,[82] and describing God's intention for marriage as a permanent union, in which two people become one flesh. He says that a man who divorces his wife and marries another commits adultery.[83]

This teaching helped to prepare the way for the Roman Catholic view that marriage is inherently indissoluble, another of those permanent changes associated with sacraments.[84] Divorce is regarded as impossible by Catholics, so the only way in which Catholics can end a marriage is by getting an annulment, which is the judgement that it was never actually a real marriage in the first place. However, this does not fit well with the teachings of Jesus.

Firstly, Jesus is well-known for his use of hyperbole in getting people to consider the state of their hearts. Anyone who looks at a woman lustfully has committed adultery with her in his heart, he says.[85] And, if your right eye causes you to sin, tear it out and throw it away.[86] No one understands this literally. Jesus himself insists that he has not come to change the law,[87] so he cannot be seen as seeking to introduce

81   Deuteronomy 24
82   Matthew 19.8
83   Matthew 19.9
84   See pp. 47-48
85   Matthew 5.27
86   Matthew 5.29
87   Matthew 5.17-18

some new legislation about divorce. Instead, he is clearly trying to get people to examine their hearts and their motives. No one who casually throws his wife out into the world and replaces her should be able to see himself as blameless.

Even with his more demanding moral logic, Jesus indicates that there are circumstances where someone is not to blame. He specifically exempts from criticism the situation where a man divorces his wife because she has been unfaithful.[88]

However, Catholic tradition adopted a more rigorous approach, insisting that divorce is always impossible. A Catholic who is abandoned by a spouse will face the agonising situation of being banned from marrying anyone else until the spouse dies, under threat of being banned from taking communion. This seems to me to be a good example of the kind of harsh religion which Jesus criticised when he complained about religious leaders who place heavy burdens on the shoulders of others.[89]

We are in an age when some people are too quick to give up on marriage, and where the greater use of counselling and pastoral support could help people to understand and care for each other better. But the Catholic approach is too harsh in completely banning all divorcees from further marriage. Elsewhere among Christian churches, divorce and remarriage is usually possible, although divorce is seen with sadness. Orthodox churches, even though they have come to share the Catholic idea that marriage is a sacrament, allow marriage for divorced people, using a form of service with a more penitential character. Practices vary among Protestant churches. But most priests in the Church of England are willing and able to conduct marriages for divorced people, having given them appropriate guidance and preparation to make sure that they are not repeating mistakes made previously.

88   Matthew 19.9
89   Matthew 23.3

SACRAMENTAL THEOLOGY

I have expressed my deepening reservations as I have gone through that Catholic list of the five additional sacraments. Some seem poorly connected with the New Testament, and some have involved over-stating the special powers of priests. Like most Protestants, I would prefer to reserve the term sacrament for baptism and the Eucharist, which seem to me to be in a category of their own. But there are many higher-church Anglicans who say things about beautiful and tradi-tional worship which I agree with, and who like to think that they can strengthen their case by talking about the seven sacraments. This seems to me to be an unnecessary and unconvincing move, involving a somewhat random list of rituals, two of which (extreme unction and confession) they mostly ignore anyway.

However, I do think that we can talk more widely about the Church and its many ceremonies as being sacramental, in a way which connects with the central Christian doctrine of the incarnation. The incarnation shows that God was happy to meet us in and through the human flesh of the person of Jesus Christ. God was pleased to do something wonderful with the material substance of our world and our human nature. And, therefore, by extension, we may expect to see God con-tinuing to do something wonderful through matter in the life of the Church. Matter is created to be good. And, though there is evil in the world, God can do things with physical stuff and with our human senses. Low-church people will tend to think that we encounter God mostly through invisible things: through prayer, through faith, and through our understanding of the Bible. High-church people tend to emphasise also that God is incarnational and sacramental. We really do meet God in and through material things and special places as he helps us to grow.

I agree with this perspective. I like the way that high-church people are often much more concerned to have churches and forms of wor-ship which are filled with beauty and which engage all of our senses and give us helpful structures to encourage our spiritual growth. The smell of incense and candles; the taste of full-bodied wine; the sound of distinctively Christian plainchant and choral polyphony; the sight of robes whose design goes back to the fourth century, silver chalices, stained glass, statues, icons, lavish decorations, and colours to highlight the drama of the seasons of the Church calendar; the soothing feel of oil; the touch of physical gestures – bowing, kneeling and genuflecting; the experience of sacred places and pilgrimages. All of these are resources which encourage us to experience and respond to the holy presence of God.

Protestants often worry that ritualism will turn into idolatry or an obsession with churchy details. And many would rightly point out that we do not need expensive robes, or silver candlesticks, or overseas pilgrimages in order to find Jesus. But I still think that there is something very meaningful in making our worship beautiful and physical and full of ways of engaging our senses.

It fascinates me that you can see something similar in the Old Testament, where God reveals long chapters of descriptions of how to build a tabernacle in the desert and then a Temple in Jerusalem, how to decorate them, how to make robes for priests, how to run all the ceremonies.[90] Then people mess it all up and forget what it all really means, and God sends prophets to say that what actually matters most is faithfulness, righteousness, mercy and love.[91] Under God's judgement, they go into exile and the Temple is destroyed,[92] leaving them struggling to worship in a foreign land.[93] But when they return, God gets them to build a new Temple and to resume all the lavish ceremonies.[94]

Jesus later criticised the corruption found in the Temple,[95] but the first Christians continued to worship there as long as they were allowed to.[96] Even the images of heavenly worship in the Book of Revelation involve elders/presbyters/priests, white robes and incense.[97] And, as soon as the Romans let them come out of hiding, the early Christians

90   e.g. Exodus 25-31, Exodus 35-40, 1 Kings 6-9
91   e.g. Amos 5.21-23, Isaiah 1.10-20
92   2 Kings 25
93   Psalm 137
94   Haggai, Ezra 3-6, Nehemiah 12
95   Mark 11.15-17
96   Acts 3.1
97   Revelation 7.9-8.5

started to build their own beautiful churches and develop more elaborate forms of worship.

The Church has developed very dramatic ways of using all of our faculties to immerse ourselves in the message of the Gospel. We re-enact the Last Supper at every Eucharist, gathering to share bread and wine as the disciples did just before Jesus' arrest. When someone is baptised by immersion, they are being buried with Christ when plunged under the water, dying to their sins, and then raised up with him to new life. In a dramatic, physical way, we become part of the story. The same is true of other aspects of Christian worship. We celebrate the incarnation, the coming of the light of Christ into the world, by the lighting of candles in dark churches in mid-winter. People go on processions on Palm Sunday to enter the experience of Jesus arriving in Jerusalem at the start of Holy Week. They wash each other's feet to remember Jesus' example of humility and love. And they sit in vigil in darkness on the night of Maundy Thursday to remember his arrest and betrayal. These actions are interwoven with a deep faith.

In lots of ways, there are outward and visible signs which enable us to ponder the invisible grace of God and to receive that grace. God, in his love for us, has chosen to draw close to us, and to allow us to experience him with our souls, our minds and our bodies.

SAINTS

To bring together the themes of this chapter, I will return to the topic of saints which I mentioned at the beginning. Faith, as I have argued, is about transformation as well as forgiveness. God is helping us to grow in love and holiness, preparing us for a greater future in a renewed world. I think that this process of sanctification can be seen very vividly in the lives of people around us and in the stories which we cherish about saints. This is what I have argued for in Chapter Five of *The Theology of Everything*. I very much value the Anglican middle way in this regard: celebrating stories of goodness without turning saints into minor deities.

Roman Catholics venerate the saints and ask them to pray for us, and I share the deep misgivings about this practice commonly expressed by

Protestants. Asking the saints to speak on our behalf makes it sound as if God himself is distant and inaccessible to us, since we need some kind of more approachable friend who will pass on a message for us. Yet the heart of Christianity is the idea that God has become one of us as Jesus Christ, dwelt among us, and that Jesus himself is now our own ambassador at the throne of God.[98]

Venerating saints and attributing special powers to them seems to me like a regression towards the more primitive polytheistic faiths which Christianity has tended to replace. People often like the idea that there is some minor deity who has a special connection to their community or to their profession or to their particular place of worship. The Catholic idea of patron saints seems to me to get worryingly close to that. When people say that St Christopher is watching over travellers, or that St George is looking out for England, I am not convinced. I think that we have some kind of unity in Christ with all of his people, living and departed, but that St Christopher has no more direct concern for me when I am on a ship than does any other Christian alive today. And any special request from me to St Christopher would have to travel via God, which seems to require the unnecessary complexity of asking God to ask St Christopher to ask God to help me.

This, of course, means that I am especially sceptical about the Catholic and Orthodox view of Mary, the mother of Jesus. Her straight-forward and trusting obedience to God has a remarkable place in the Bible, is a deeply inspiring example, and plays a crucial role in God's dealings with the world.[99] But Catholic tradition has gone to extraordi-nary extremes in its enthusiasm for Mary, perhaps fuelled by a tendency at times to make God seem too remote and emotionally detached. The story of Mary in the New Testament is of an ordinary young woman who was willing to serve God, and whose own body provided the means for God to share in our humanity and to be born as one of us. The fact that divinity dwelt fully in her womb and that she fed the eternal Word of God from her breasts is a vivid and astonishing affirmation of the incarnation. But it diminishes that account of divinity and humanity

98   see Hebrews 4.14-16
99   Luke 1.26-56

joining together if we embroider it with ideas that Mary herself had spe-cial divine powers and was anything other than a normal human being.

Early in the history of the Church, legends developed that Mary was an aristocrat who had grown up in the Temple in Jerusalem. Then there were myths that her body was completely unaffected by childbirth, and Catholic tradition came to assert that she remained a virgin for the rest of her life, despite her marriage to Joseph. The Gospels mention Jesus' brothers,[100] so that tradition is forced to conclude that these must have been cousins or step-brothers.

Further developments said that Mary herself had been conceived in a miraculous way, the doctrine of the Immaculate Conception, which meant that she had not inherited original sin, unlike all of her ances-tors. Finally, it was said that she had not even died in the usual way, but had been assumed bodily into heaven and crowned as its Queen. These two Catholic doctrines were proclaimed as infallible dogmas by popes in 1854 and 1950. Other Catholics have suggested going further in describing Mary as sharing in Jesus's role as mediator between God and people.

Protestants get very annoyed or just utterly baffled by these ideas, which provide a very good example of the need for Christian tradition to be compatible with Scripture. I think that if Mary had been assumed into heaven in the first century and crowned as its Queen, then the New Testament would say so. It would have been understood at the time as an event which was worth mentioning, rather than gradually emerging over the centuries afterwards. Instead, the role of Mary seems to dimin-ish during the New Testament. When people excitedly tell Jesus that his mother and brothers are waiting outside, he replies that his mother and brothers are anyone who hears the word of God and obeys it.[101]

Protestants are right to challenge these flights of fancy about Mary and the saints, but they then mostly seem to me to overreact. There is a strong Protestant tendency to ignore Mary, and to pay no atten-tion to the lives of those who have lived between the New Testament and today. When we understand salvation as being primarily about

100 Matthew 12.46
101 Matthew 12.46-50

forgiveness, that approach makes sense. Mary and all other Christians are simply forgiven sinners, deserving of hell but received graciously by God into his Kingdom.

However, I do take the Catholic side in saying that salvation is primarily about the forming of people in relationships of love with God and each other. And so the stories of the earthly lives of holy people, through which the Holy Spirit trained them to become like Jesus, are fascinating and important.[102] Those stories should be cherished and celebrated and used to inspire us, without then making any suggestion that those same holy people are now able to respond to our prayers. This is the middle way taken by the Church of England in celebrating the lives of saints, without treating them as minor deities. We have a calendar which tells the stories of many significant heroes of the faith day by day, celebrating their examples so that they can inspire and encourage us.[103] On 1 November, we celebrate the feast of All Saints, which gives us a chance to think of all those who have lived holy lives without becoming famous. Many other Protestants would be nervous about these celebrations, preferring to return to their familiar emphasis on the sinfulness of all people. But it seems to me that God really does inspire and enable people to grow and to change, and that we should notice that work of grace and be excited about it.

CONCLUSION

In this chapter, I have sought to draw on the best aspects of the Catholic and Protestant understandings of salvation. It is all based on forgiveness, as the Protestants insist: on an act of love and affirmation that comes from God, and which is far beyond anything which we could manufacture or earn for ourselves. But God leads us on a spiritual journey of transformation, as the Catholics insist, bringing about a real change in us which is meaningful and necessary, and which leads on to a closer union with God in the life to come. God's grace is freely

---

102   I have written more about this view of saints at the end of Chapter Five of *The Theology of Everything*

103   In daily prayers in my college chapel, we read the brief biographies of the saints from Brother Tristram SSF, ed (2003) *Exciting Holiness* Canterbury Press

offered to all individuals, as the Protestants insist, without needing to be tightly regulated by clergy and without being dependent on our own heroic efforts. But faith is about more than initial conversion, as the Catholics insist, and the Church holds a vast treasury of resources and wisdom to help us along our journey in spiritual and practical ways.

Christian worship is sacramental, in that the Holy Spirit makes use of physical matter in order to engage with our senses, so that we may encounter God through bread, wine, water, music and art in places and ceremonies which are full of an experience of holiness and beauty. In particular, the beginning of the Christian life is marked by baptism, most vividly seen in the immersion of an adult under water who is identifying with the death and resurrection of Jesus. And the journey of faith is sustained week by week through the Sunday Eucharist, in which we meet Christ in the blessing and sharing of bread and wine, experiencing his offering of himself for us on the cross. Those great themes are further explored by many other sacred actions: the ashes of repentance at the start of Lent, the carrying of palm crosses at the start of Holy Week, the lighting of fires in the darkness at Easter, the exchange of rings in the marriage service, the laying on of hands with prayers for confirmation or to set aside and equip someone for a new ministry. All of those actions and many others help us to grow in the life of faith described in the Bible, as we ponder its words and seek to live as disciples of Jesus. Following this journey of faith, we join with all the saints who have gone before us, so that we also are gradually able to become an inspiration and support to those around us today and in the future.

Through the histories of the lives of the saints we see signs of the work of the Holy Spirit over the last two thousand years. In many cases, we can use prayers and hymns that they wrote centuries ago in our services today. But some Christians look to the past to find out how to worship, while others expect the Spirit to be guiding the reinvention of worship today. In the next chapter, we arrive at one of the questions which most deeply divides Christians today.

SUGGESTIONS FOR FURTHER READING

Andrew Davison's *Why Sacraments?* (2013, SPCK) is written from an Anglo-Catholic perspective, giving a clear and accessible account of the seven sacraments.

From the other perspective, Philip Yancey's *What's So Amazing About Grace* (2002, Zondervan) has found a very enthusiastic reception among Protestants, emphasising God's free gift of forgiveness found without reference to rules, ceremonies or hierarchies.

For more about the Church of England's celebration of the lives of holy people, see *Saints on Earth: A Biographical Companion to Common Worship* by John H Darch and Stuart K Burns (2017, Church House Publishing).

Chapter Four
Worship:
Traditional and Contemporary

In most ordinary local churches, one kind of argument has usually been the fiercest. It is about whether we should keep the old wooden pews or have some comfy new upholstered chairs; whether we should have traditional hymns accompanied by the organ or the latest worship songs led by a guitarist; whether the minister should wear robes and a clerical collar, climbing the pulpit steps to preach, or should be in jeans and an open-necked shirt, strolling around casually on a stage with a microphone; whether children should learn to sit patiently in silence, or should be allowed to run around noisily; and whether the prayers and readings should address God as 'thou' or 'you'.

This is an argument which has cut across nearly all denominations. Only the Orthodox have avoided it completely, since they are unshakable in their belief that nothing has a serious claim to be Christian unless it has been around for a millennium or more. But, gathering pace since about 1970, a drive to make all things seem modern, relevant and lively has swept across most Catholic and Protestant churches. On the whole, the modernisers have won, in that most churches have changed dramatically.

If we look back to 60 years ago, church services were very different. Anglicans, even the Evangelical ones, would all expect their clergy to be in robes, would all be familiar with the 16th-century words of the *Book of Common Prayer*, and would all feel at home singing *Glorious things of thee are spoken* accompanied by a Victorian pipe organ. Other

Protestants who had no robes or liturgy would be still dressed up in their smartest suits on Sundays, and would go to churches which had pews and stained glass and an air of dignity, where the preacher might be in a black academic gown and clerical collar. Over in the Catholic Church, services consisted mostly of Latin spoken by a priest at the altar surrounded by incense with his back to the congregation, swathed in an atmosphere of mystery and wonder. Church for all Christians conveyed a sense of stability, order, holiness, reverence and awe.

But Western society from the 1960s began to enjoy a surge of new prosperity, new freedoms, and sexual liberation, in which teenagers took the lead in forming lively new youth cultures. People went to the moon, flew in supersonic jets, watched more and more TV, began to use computers, experimented with various mind-altering substances, and acquired the habit of carrying around portable pop music using a succession of new technologies. In this world, churches began to seem fossilised, stuffy, over-authoritarian, irrelevant, dull, repressed and unhealthy.

Devout Christians admired some of the hopefulness and joyful spontaneity which they saw in the culture around them. Many wondered how many of their inherited church traditions were worth keeping. Was Jesus to be found in a cold, stone building, sitting on a hard pew under a gothic archway listening to tired old men speaking Latin or Tudor English? Or was he outside with the crowds, in the marketplaces, in the discos, among the poor, and with the guitar-players singing songs about social justice?

Some of them sought urgently to update the Church's theology, including raising the questions about our ways of describing God in the light of modern science which I have explored in *The Theology of Everything*. Many tried to update the Church's social teachings, raising other questions which I will be discussing in the later chapters of this book. But the most obvious manifestation of the spirit of the 1970s has been a drive to liven up Christian worship, making it more informal and more similar to popular culture. Out went the robed choirs and organs, in came the guitars and contemporary worship songs. Out went the pews and in came the comfy chairs and hotel carpets. Out went the dignified and carefully-considered liturgical words used for many centuries, and in came a chatty spontaneity reminiscent of TV talk shows and local radio.

Much genuine excitement and revival of church life followed. Great effort went into making churches more warm and welcoming, which was a very worthwhile exercise. There was often a new liveliness, energy and sense of purpose which was in itself attractive and helpful. Instead of unthinkingly repeating old customs, there was an outpouring of new creativity and a new awareness of the need to connect with those who were not going to church.

People looked long and hard at the old liturgies and wondered if they were really still serving their purpose. The Catholic Mass was rewritten and translated into people's ordinary languages, so that the message of the Scriptures could be heard and understood. Church of England services stopped sounding like Shakespeare and began to use ordinary modern English. And a lot of shared interdenominational scholarship led to new Protestant and Catholic liturgies which shared many of the same words.

Across a wide range of churches, this process of modernisation was felt to be essential, and a very broad spectrum of Western church leaders continue to believe with great conviction that the process has further to go. Everything must be made jollier and more casual and better-adapted to the attention span of small children. I keep hearing from clergy who are still earnestly convinced that even more cheerfulness, even more discarding of tradition, even more copying of the casual chattiness of breakfast TV shows will lead us forward into church growth. Lots of my colleagues are still putting their energy into things called *new ways of being church*, or the *emerging church*, seeking to grow new forms of Christian community as cafes or children's *messy church* clubs. They see traditional services as something which can be kept going while there are enough stubborn elderly people who like them, but which will soon die out.

Every effort to be welcoming and to build community is very worthwhile and is likely to bear some fruit. But trying to take this modernisation programme even further seems to me to be like trying to squeeze water from a sponge that is nearly dry. Informal approaches have been very comprehensively explored and do not have much left to offer. Among the students I work with, informal worship with guitars and contemporary songs may attract a handful of enthusiasts who have grown up with that sort of thing. But the best way of filling our Chapel is to hold a Compline: a late-night, candlelit liturgy based on the final service of the day in medieval monasteries, consisting mainly of Gregorian chant sung in Tudor English or Latin by a choir wearing black gowns. It is a service which talks honestly about good and evil in very stark language, as well as delivering an extraordinary sense of stillness, unhurried calm and beauty. It provides a sense of the sacred which feels completely different from ordinary life. To young people who have been brought up without a faith, informality can look like a weak and cringe-making imitation of secular culture. However, an authentic taste of a traditional spirituality is starting to seem much more interesting again.

My experience has led me to become increasingly sceptical of what I am mischievously labelling the spirit of the 1970s, which is so dominant in today's churches. My claim to be taking a central approach in this chapter therefore involves taking my bearings from the history of the Church as a whole, without confining myself to the anomalies of the last half-century. But first, I will take a look at the main manifestations of the contemporary Church's love of informality.

THE STRUGGLES OF MODERN CATHOLICISM

I have been to many Catholic Masses while travelling around Europe, and have found that the experience tends to go to one of two extremes. Anything involving members of a religious community is often extraordinarily graceful, with a tangible atmosphere of deep prayer. The spiritual life of nuns and monks can be a privilege to glimpse. Otherwise, today's Catholic Masses are usually a remarkably disappointing experience, even in the most spectacular of cathedrals. People who only know about Catholicism through historical TV dramas might be quite surprised if they went along to an ordinary Sunday Mass in a Catholic parish church.

Today's Catholicism has lost most of the sense of awe, mystery, grandeur and beauty of the old Latin services. But Catholics have somehow never learned to join in enthusiastically with the modern services which were devised to encourage congregational participation. Catholics have not acquired the Protestant love of singing rousing hymns with gusto, nor of speaking together in confident unison. Instead, they tend to mumble their congregational parts of the liturgy at a diverse set of high speeds. Even taking communion happens in a hurry, with little sense of lingering over an important experience: just the very efficient dispensing of wafers to people standing in a fast-moving queue. I find all of it a very odd way of doing things which is neither grand and glorious nor warm and joyful.

In most Catholic churches, the prevailing aesthetic for robes and altar frontals and other decorations is one which reminds me of 1970s children's story books: a kind of cheerful minimalism with solid bright colours and strangely angular depictions of fishes and ears of corn. It looks weirdly dated to my eyes. But for Roman Catholics who are more liberal, this style of art is part of the fiercely guarded symbolism of the great hope of an updated Catholicism that began in the 1960s.

I have already mentioned the Second Vatican Council (1962-5) several times. This meeting of all the world's Catholic bishops was the first since the very defiant First Vatican Council (1869-70) proclaimed the dogma of papal infallibility. Vatican II was called by Pope John XXIII (reigned 1958-1963), who expressed a desire to 'throw open the windows of the Church and let the fresh air of the Spirit blow through.' It turned the Catholic Church in a much more Protestant direction, encouraging the study of the Bible, recognising Protestants as genuine Christians, affirming freedom of religion, seeking ecumenical unity and being ready to affirm the goodness found in other religions and philosophies. It called for a revision of the Mass which would involve far greater congregational participation, including the use of today's languages rather than Latin.

The new Mass was introduced in 1970, and carried with it an energetic movement of updating Catholic churches. This was often controversial, and arguably owed more to something popularly known as the *spirit* of Vatican II rather than to the letter of the Council documents themselves. I mentioned the rearrangement of churches in the last chapter, which enabled the priest to face the people across an altar which was now reacquiring the symbolism of a dining table. This change was accompanied by the radical simplification of ceremonies, the introduction of more contemporary music, the clearing out of all things gothic and medieval, and the bringing in of that odd 1970s children's story book aesthetic.

A lot was at stake in this movement, as many Catholics were hoping for further progress in a Protestant and a liberal direction. Their hopes had been partly disappointed by the 1968 papal encyclical which reaffirmed the Catholic rejection of artificial contraception (a subject which I will return to in Chapter Six). But many older Catholics were bewildered by the rapid changes which had already taken place to their churches and patterns of worship.

The Catholic Church is therefore still absorbing the consequences of Vatican II with some continuing indigestion. Pope Benedict XVI (reigned 2005-2013) sought to move the Catholic Church in a more cautious and traditionalist direction, bringing back the option of the traditional Latin Mass and all its elaborate ceremonial in 2007. The English translation of the new Mass was also revised in 2011 to make it closer to the Latin text, and further away from the ecumenical versions which had been shared so optimistically with Anglicans and others. But his successor Pope Francis (since 2013) has a habit of alarming traditionalists with his rather more relaxed and spontaneous approach to liturgy, and now in 2021 has restricted access to the old Latin Mass again.

From my perspective, Vatican II was largely a very good thing (especially in the friendlier approach taken to Protestants), but I think that the dramatic shift in Catholic worship style was too big a leap to work well, and that much of the glory of the old Catholic liturgy has been lost.

Mine is not a perspective which would fit tidily into the factions of the Catholic Church, as those who would join me in a love of Latin plainchant and beautiful liturgies tend to be the ones whose theological views I might find rather reactionary. In the Roman Catholic Church, the badge of those moves towards Protestantism and liberalism is a style of worship which I find rather disappointing. But in Anglican circles, it is much more possible to be enjoy the splendours of traditional worship at the same time as being a supporter of developments such as the ordination of women. Many Anglo-Catholics have continued to use the old medieval Catholic-style ceremonial in all of its glory, irrespective of whether they are liberal in their other views. In England, a traditional Catholic approach to worship is now much easier to find among Anglo-Catholics (both liberal and conservative) than among Roman Catholics.

Here is one interesting comparison. It is normal in most of the Church of England for people to kneel down to receive communion. We walk up to the altar, kneel at a communion rail, and spend some peaceful, prayerful time there, humbly holding our hands out in front of us, while the consecrated bread is offered to us and then the wine. We pause for a while before standing again. It is an experience of quietly seeking to be fed and nurtured by God, and a sign that something sacred is happening. We have been doing it this way for 500 years, when we continued the medieval Catholic tradition of kneeling, extending the experience by restoring the early Church's practice of offering the wine to the laity.

Yet in today's Catholic church, following the reforms of the 60s and 70s, people usually just quickly receive a wafer standing up. For any progressive Catholic, kneeling is associated with the dark old days, and is interpreted as a sign of being opposed to any further reforms. I once knew a Catholic student who was campaigning for the ordination of women: she loved much about the Church of England, but thought that kneeling at communion was a shocking medieval abomination, and always remained standing on principle. Sadly, it is difficult for Catholics to enjoy all of their heritage in worship if they are not also very conservative in relation to modern social changes.

OVERLOADED LECTIONARIES
AND RAMBLING SERMONS

Another change brought by Vatican II has involved the use of the Bible in services. For most of the history of the Roman Catholic Church, the Bible was never heard in the language of the ordinary people. Every Mass would have two readings, repeating on a one-year cycle, both of which were in Latin. From 1970, a very ambitious new scheme was created in order to pump a high volume of Scripture past Catholics, as a dramatic step of repentance for the previous drought. Readings were now in the local contemporary language, and every Mass included an Old Testament reading, a Psalm, a New Testament reading and a Gospel reading. A colossal new three-year lectionary was constructed, covering a much greater proportion of the Bible. This new love of Scripture won the applause of some Protestant denominations, including the Church of England, who spotted a good opportunity for ecumenical alignment by adopting their own versions of the new Catholic three-year cycle of readings.

Sadly, I think this enthusiastic leap in a Protestant direction has been rather like the Catholic attempts to encourage congregational participation: well-intentioned, but limited in its success. This great flood of Scripture is not the way that well-designed services have usually worked in most Protestant churches, which have normally looked at one Bible reading at a time. Perhaps there is another passage which helps to set the scene for it or complements it, but usually a Protestant sermon focuses very strongly on one text, and often the hymns and prayers in that service will have been chosen to fit the same teaching theme. Often that sermon is part of a series so that, for example, a church might spend a couple of months reflecting on one book of the Bible. This makes for a coherent series of services which has a clear impact on people, who get to the end feeling that they have understood something.

Since 1970, however, Catholics have suffered from scriptural indigestion, which has spread to many Anglicans and others. The three readings may have little connection with each other, just being the next instalments in three separate strands of Biblical narrative, joined with a loosely connected Psalm. Very few members of the congregation will successfully keep track of all the storylines or threads of argument, or remember anything about their context from week to week. But the bizarre assumption has arisen in many places that it is the task of the preacher each Sunday to reflect on all of them at once. It is like having to search for a connecting theme in this week's episodes of *The Crown*, *Doctor Who* and *EastEnders*. I despair of this approach, and try very hard to encourage trainee clergy to resist it. It leads to convoluted and rambling sermons which are like some strange party game in which contestants have to join up multiple unrelated texts, thereby failing to listen closely to any one of them. The result can help to provoke some gentle musings by the congregation, but it often leaves them with no clear sense that there was any particular message buried in the midst of it all. Sometimes the preacher may have mercifully focused on one reading, but then the organist may have chosen the hymns based on another, and the person leading the intercessions may have felt most inspired by the themes of the third. The combination is frequently rather incoherent.

I mention this in the context of the spirit of the 1970s because I think that this overdose of Scripture has actually often enabled an avoidance of engaging deeply with the Bible, allowing liturgical churches to take refuge in being cheerfully bland and inoffensive. It provides the perfect cover for preachers who are happy to waffle on about some parallels in poetry and symbolism for ten minutes, while avoiding saying anything that is definite enough to run the risk of provoking any kind of serious thought or debate.

In my view, there are two approaches to using Scriptures in worship which are far more meaningful. One is a carefully-planned series of sermons exploring one biblical book at a time, as I have already mentioned. Some good suggested programmes can be found in the Church of England's *New Patterns for Worship*. The other is the ancient lectionary of the western Church, which has tragically now been almost entirely forgotten. It took shape in the first millennium and provided the one-year cycle of readings which the Catholics were using in Latin until 1970, and which the Church of England was using in English until 1980 by printing it in full in the *Book of Common Prayer* (where it still remains as a mostly forgotten resource). One of the things that the Reformers did not change was this lectionary, which they agreed gave a reliable journey through the main themes of the Scriptures. Each week has two readings and an associated prayer (the Collect), which connect together in very powerful ways. The familiarity gained by their repetition year by year provides a useful framework for preaching and for worship, giving everyone a strong shared basis for their own further explorations of the Scriptures. The Orthodox still have their own historic one-year lectionary. But sadly, very few of the enthusiasts for liturgy found among Catholics and higher-church Protestants can now remember that this is the way that liturgy was actually designed to work.

EVANGELICALS AND CHARISMATICS

I turn now to the effects of the spirit of the 1970s on the lower parts of the Church, which have displayed their own great commitment to the modernisation of worship. Two different perspectives can be found among two different kinds of Evangelical.

All Evangelicals emphasise the central importance of the Bible as the place where we find divine revelation, but today's Charismatics see their faith in rather more emotional and experiential terms than others, expecting to feel aware of the miraculous work of the Holy Spirit. Since the early days of Evangelicalism, there have always been many who felt that the Bible pointed to a Christian life which was emotional, full of a vivid awareness of the guidance of the Holy Spirit, prompting tears of repentance and a joyful sense of the love of God. For others, there has been less interest in human experiences and feelings, and a more sober sense that the Bible gives us an objective account of the grace of God which is independent of our changeable emotional state. When it comes to the great modernisation of worship, these two approaches point in somewhat different directions.

The Charismatic renewal movement began in 1960 as an upsurge of Pentecostal enthusiasm within the historic denominations, before spilling over into the creation of new churches. Charismatics emphasise the encounter with the miraculous power of the Holy Spirit in the present moment, especially within very lively and highly emotional services. Charismatics expect to find the authentic work of the Holy Spirit in experiences which seem new and spontaneous, and think that faithfulness to traditions is more likely to involve getting stuck in a rut of dull human habits.

Charismatic churches may come and go surprisingly rapidly: planting, splitting, merging, renaming themselves and changing venue, energetically conveying a belief that they are following the very latest move of the Spirit. Charismatic worship songs are like pop music: a small number become long-term classics, but the genre mostly consists of new compositions which are sung with great excitement for a short time by people who like to think that they are being truly prophetic in keeping up to date with the latest forms of Spirit-filled worship.

To my mind, the greatest contribution of Charismatics has been the affirmation of the spiritual gifts of all lay-people, getting away from the sense that everything in church life is entirely dependent on the clergy. This has attracted a lot of attention to important New Testament teachings about the importance of the talents and vocations of everyone.[104] Deeper experiences of Christian community and discipleship have been inspired by the Charismatic movement, both within existing denominations and in new fellowships. Much good has resulted.

But there have been problems. Charismatics, in my experience, tend to develop strange bubbles of triumphalist expectation, holding exciting worship sessions and conferences in which they convince each other that incredible things have been happening elsewhere in the world and are just about to happen here. There is always said to be a great revival just around the corner, when the Holy Spirit will soon bring vast numbers flocking into the Church. I first encountered that belief in 1990 when a group called the Kansas City Prophets proclaimed that the revival was just about to begin in Britain. It did not. Then there was the Toronto Blessing of 1994, which sent a great wave of Charismatic excitement and expectation around the world. I remember a preacher telling an excited congregation that we would each have to lead a new church when the revival came. That did not happen either. But there

104   e.g. 1 Corinthians 12, Ephesians 4.1-16, and see pp. 71-72

were always stories about thousands of people coming to faith all of a sudden, stories which somehow always seemed to come from distant and inaccessible parts of the world.

Charismatics can be very enthusiastic about prayers for healing, especially within very emotionally-charged services of worship, sometimes encouraging adrenaline-filled invalids to climb out of their wheelchairs or throw away their crutches. Some of this is quite blatantly fraudulent, including a notorious set of tricks deployed to make people think that inequalities in the lengths of their legs are being evened out. Much of the rest is hype and wishful thinking, with a conspicuous shortage of medical evidence for lasting miraculous cures.

Since the movement relies much more on emotional punch and eager anticipation than on any careful reflection, there is a lack of good, thoughtful Charismatic theology. The biggest omission, in my view, is the failure to realise that if God is guiding us so powerfully in the present moment then he must have been guiding the Church very powerfully throughout its history. It seems to me that Charismatic Christianity must point logically towards some kind of Catholic Christianity which takes tradition seriously. Many people like me who have enjoyed Charismatic churches in our early days as Christians have grown away from them, moving in search of something with deeper roots in historic theology and spirituality. In some ways the Charismatic experience seems to me like the crazy excitement of the early stages of being in love: either it will mature into something deeper, steadier and more realistic, or it will fizzle out and leave a restless longing to begin the same experience again in a new setting. I mostly gave up on the Charismatic movement when I got tired of the unrealistic triumphalism, and concluded that being a Christian today involved asking much harder questions about our place in a Western society which is moving away from faith.

For those who continue to delight in Charismatic Christianity, there has been a great synergy between the informal and hedonistic spirit of the 1970s and the belief that the work of the Holy Spirit is something immediate, exciting and miraculous. This is likely to last for a long while to come. However, for less emotional Evangelicals, their current love of informality is more a matter of temporary convenience than of any great theological conviction.

The conservative Evangelicals who put their emphasis on a calmer encounter with the Holy Scriptures are happy for now to embrace a relaxed, jeans-wearing vibe and the use of contemporary music styles, while this approach helps people to see past old assumptions about boring churches and inspires them to listen to the preaching of the Gospel. My guess is that this factor this will start to tip the other way before much longer, as the aping of popular culture begins to appear more and more tired and unconvincing. The riches of the early Protestant liturgies in the *Book of Common Prayer* with their deep and beautiful engagement with Scripture are ready to be rediscovered. As soon as the Evangelical movement realises that Church can capture people's attention by being different from today's world and more rooted in things that last, I predict that a return to stillness and reverence and liturgy will be on its way.

THE EMERGING CHURCH

Among more liberal Protestants, another very natural partnership has developed between a bottom-up view of the Church and the spirit of the 1970s. It has some roots in Evangelicalism but is moving away from traditional ways of equipping congregations for the work of mission, preferring a broader, gentler and less prescriptive set of approaches.

This very diverse and decentralised movement is often called the *emerging church*. It is happy to question all of the traditional structures of both high and low churches. Parishes, buildings, gothic architecture, clergy, Sunday worship, robes, liturgies, sermons, sacraments, systematic theologies, traditional hymns, modern worship songs and evangelistic campaigns may all be seen as optional: they are the trappings of churchiness formed in a more authoritarian and judgemental age. Enthusiasts for a new approach may call themselves things like *post-Evangelical*, *post-liberal* or *postmodern*, or avoid labels completely. They are likely to talk enthusiastically about *new ways of being church*, or *fresh expressions*, or *pioneer ministry*. They often have an Evangelical background, but may have come to regard the usual expressions of

Evangelicalism as too aggressive, too judgemental, too inward-looking, too socially conservative, or just too dull.

In this lowest of all low-church approaches, seeking the emerging church means somehow nurturing Christian life and community in a way which is authentic and natural for the world we now live in. It assumes that there is some kind of a true core of Christianity which is the message of Jesus, which can be liberated from all the traditional unpacking of that message in terms of patterns of worship, theologies and leadership structures.

So the emerging church might mean a group of people meeting up in a local café on a Wednesday afternoon, if that is what is convenient for them, and developing their own informal way of praying together and supporting each other in their faith. Or it might mean a lunchtime gathering at a particular workplace, or something associated with a hobby or local community project. Other emerging church people might still hold Sunday services but explore *alternative worship*, perhaps involving various interactive prayer stations with tealights, pebbles, bowls of water and Post-it notes, where people move around the building as individuals exploring different expressions of faith, without ever singing together or listening together.

This sort of thing seems to me to be quite reasonable and worthwhile as a set of activities that happen on the edges of church life. But I have become rather sceptical about the grandiose claims made by some of those who think that they are the very cool pioneers of a more authentic and relevant expression of Christianity. The emerging church shares with the Charismatic movement that unconvincing habit of suggesting that great and wondrous things are just about to happen. As far as I can see, not very much of any substance has actually emerged yet. I once read a very exciting account of an amazing new group which was holding informal gatherings in houses based around a fellowship lunch which was partly a celebration of holy communion. The account made it sound very genuine, welcoming and deeply connected with its local community. It happened to be near where I was working at the time, so I asked to visit it. To my astonishment, the group turned out to be a small collection of church ministers, theology lecturers and their spouses. It just seemed like a fairly ordinary midweek church fellowship group to me, and was clearly entirely dependent on the foundation that its members had already received from their very extensive experience of more traditional church life.

My guess is that nothing of any great significance is going to emerge from this movement, although I would be delighted to be proved wrong. Lots of very good and worthwhile prayer meetings, fellowship groups and community events have been held under its diverse set of banners, but the Church has always done those kinds of thing in some way. Every emerging expression of faith is still dependent on a much more traditional infrastructure of clergy, theological colleges, parishes, buildings, sermons and sacraments. Nothing has ever taken root as an organic replacement to those older resources and structures, and it is highly misleading to suggest that it is just about to. And so I finally return to the territory which the spirit of the 1970s dismissed as outdated and irrelevant.

THE STRENGTH AND BEAUTY
OF TRADITIONAL WORSHIP

In 2011, my mother died suddenly and unexpectedly of a massive brain haemorrhage, just as I was beginning the new academic year at work. It was a very difficult time for me, and I mostly wanted to try to continue as usual, surrounded by bright young students. I kept my usual routine of services going, which helped. But the more modern expressions of Christian faith began to seem hollow, flimsy and unreal. The safety net that caught me was the words of the funeral service from the *Book of Common Prayer*. The first ones that came to mind were sentences which I had sung with the chapel choir, set to music by Henry Purcell (1659-95):

> Man that is born of a woman hath but a short time to live, and is full of misery. He cometh up, and is cut down, like a flower; he fleeth as it were a shadow, and never continueth in one stay.

> In the midst of life we are in death: of whom may we seek for succour, but of thee, O Lord, who for our sins art justly displeased?

Yet, O Lord God most holy, O Lord most mighty, O holy and
most merciful Saviour, deliver us not into the bitter pains of
eternal death.

Thou knowest, Lord, the secrets of our hearts; shut not thy
merciful ears to our prayer; but spare us, Lord most holy, O
God most mighty, O holy and merciful Saviour, thou most
worthy Judge eternal, suffer us not, at our last hour, for any
pains of death, to fall from thee.

For a long time, I had been wary of the sternness of such words, with
their uncompromising account of frailty, mortality, sin and judgement.
I had preferred modern liturgies which were brighter, more affirming,
more upbeat, and more encouraging. But when bereavement suddenly
slammed into my life with no warning, that sombre, poignant and
majestic 16th-century text was the only thing in my head which could
begin to grapple with the enormity of the experience.

Reading further through the service, I came across a verse from
Psalm 90 which I found myself wanting to repeat over and over in the
weeks and months that followed.

The days of our age are threescore years and ten; and though
men be so strong, that they come to fourscore years : yet is their
strength then but labour and sorrow; so soon passeth it away,
and we are gone.

We buried my mother's ashes on the day when she would have
completed her fourscore years, and I thought about the various health
problems which had made her very frail in her last decade. The verse
seemed to fit her struggles and her departure very closely. But I also felt
that every time I said those words, I was somehow standing with five
centuries of people who had mourned for their loved ones in exactly
the same way, and with three thousand years of Jews and Christians
who had used that Psalm in various other versions as they confronted
the horror of mortality.

What I realised then very powerfully was that it meant more to
me than I could ever describe to feel that I was part of a very long and
deeply-rooted tradition. I was not facing this darkness on my own, but

others had been here before and had left some signposts to show that they had got through it and that their prayers had sustained them. It meant that the life of faith had a well-trodden pathway through this experience of rage and loss and regret and loneliness.

I have come to love the *Book of Common Prayer* far more than I ever thought possible, including its monthly journey through all of the Psalms in its daily services. They are uncompromising in their engagement with the nastier experiences of life, as well as its joys. They express guilt and sorrow very profoundly and with a raw honesty, alongside an unflinching sense of the grandeur of God. When Jesus was dying on the cross, it was the words of Psalm 22 which came to his lips – 'My God, my God, why have you forsaken me?' This is what good liturgy does to us: it seeps into us, day by day, year by year, and then speaks within us at those times when we are otherwise completely unprepared.

I do not just mean that old things are good at expressing gloom or dealing with emergencies. Handel's *Hallelujah Chorus,* Tallis's *Spem in Alium,* or Parry's *I was glad* are fabulous examples of choral settings of biblical texts in traditional versions which have been handed on to us because of their surpassing excellence in elevating the human spirit in worship. There is a long and careful process of passing on the most inspiring examples of each generation's expressions of faith, and we can see examples from recent decades taking their place in that great tradition. But we miss out on so much if we assume that only the newest and most immediately accessible words and music are worth noticing.

The quest for authentic and up to date worship can involve an endless struggle to forge something that fits our current situation perfectly, like trying to express this week's Twitter trends and the very latest correct opinions on the issues of the day. The danger is that we shape something around ourselves so well that it merely carries our own image, and has no ability to disturb us or enlarge our perspective. There are passages in the *Book of Common Prayer* which I would be very happy to tone down, but there is also something very powerful about a text from another age which is so deeply immersed in words and themes from the Bible. It does not have to sound like some agreed statement produced by a committee which everyone can agree with: it can keep its own sense of strangeness or even offensiveness. We can use it because it is our inheritance, and because it has the ability both to reassure us and to disturb us, without having to claim that it is the perfect expression of what we all think this week.

The unchanging rhythms of traditional services can also help us to stop being frantic and anxious and excessively preoccupied with many things, guiding us carefully through an experience of worship which does not have to fit our own agenda. And, as with my experience of bereavement, even their extreme and surprising corners may suddenly one day turn out to be more relevant than anything else in the world.

The informality and restless innovation of the last 50 years is an anomaly in Church history. The great majority of Christians through history have worshipped in beautiful buildings, have used robes and special music and historic liturgies, and have used forms of language which intentionally carry a sense of weight and tradition, rather than trying to sound like popular culture. These resources are found abundantly within the heritage of the Church of England, as well as in many other denominations.

Far too little attention has yet been paid to the fact that one of the greatest success stories in the Church of England in recent years is our cathedrals, where a traditional choral style of worship has continued and flourished. Congregations throughout the week have been growing, because the combination of beautiful music, traditional liturgy and thoughtful preaching is one which seems worthwhile and meaningful to an increasing number of people. A style of worship which has been widely abandoned by parishes is attracting new followers in these centres of excellence.

Now is the time, it seems to me, to put lot of energy into re-establishing church choirs, enjoying the beauty and majesty of the riches of our traditions, all combined with hospitality and helpful preaching, refusing to dumb anything down, but providing avenues of exploration for everyone. It is possible, I would argue, to combine an enjoyment of the best of our traditions with a very warm welcome to newcomers and with an openness to ways in which the Church needs to continue to develop. But in recent years it has mostly been those energetically updating worship who have tried the hardest to make newcomers welcome and to explain to them what is going on. Whereas the people who run traditional churches have often retreated defensively, and have struggled to believe that anyone new might be genuinely interested.

But warm attitudes to newcomers are not inherently linked to informality. My experience of running a college chapel with a beautiful building and a talented choir is that it is perfectly possible to combine that tradition with a strong emphasis on hospitality, welcome and an enthusiasm for answering people's questions. We have candlelit services with some of the best music from the last five hundred years or more. And we also have talks and discussions, with lots to eat and drink, where I engage with students' questions and lead them deeper into an understanding of the Christian faith.

I think that today's young people are not put off the Church because of its traditions, but simply assume that it is not for them because they have no experience or understanding of it. Trying to make it comfy and modern just makes it look like a pale imitation of a TV show. But something that is deeply rooted in the best traditions of our civilisation is something which they can find fascinating, when we make them welcome and help them to see what is going on. An experience of contemplation, stillness and of a tradition which is at peace with itself can be a rare and inspiring encounter. It also helps to have good coffee, well-produced service booklets, and a willingness to listen and to explain things with warmth and patience.

Finally, I would say that this love of tradition does not require being closed to all change and innovation. During the coronavirus lockdown of 2020, we moved our chapel services online, and were thereby able to continue holding daily Morning and Evening Prayer. One such occasion while I was working on this chapter involved us using the 1560 version of the *Book of Common Prayer* in Latin, when I was joined on Zoom by an engineering student in Argentina, a classicist in the United States and a theoretical chemist in Cambridge. We found that the best form of music for videoconference services is traditional plainchant sung by solo voices. New technologies, new challenges and traditional resources can all fit together in surprising ways. From the centre, the best of the high and the low can be enjoyed.

SUGGESTIONS FOR FURTHER READING

For a good taste of charismatic spirituality and an inspiring vision of worship which is informal, emotional and seeks to be guided by the Holy Spirit, see *Why Worship? Insights into the Wonder of Worship* edited by Tim Hughes and Nick Drake with Liza Hoeksma (2021, SPCK).

For a 'flexible, fluid way of being church', full of spontaneity and creativity, see *Liquid Church* by Pete Ward (2013, Wipf and Stock).

And for the idea that informal fresh expressions of church can emerge in all kinds of social contexts, see *Being Church, Doing Life: Creating Gospel Communities where Life Happens* Michael Moynagh (2014, Monarch).

For the opposite perspective, emphasising the traditional structures of the Church, see *For the Parish: A Critique of Fresh Expressions* by Andrew Davison and Alison Milbank (2010, SCM).

A fascinating and strongly argued case for the Traditional Latin Mass is presented by Peter Kwasniewski in *Reclaiming Our Roman Catholic Birthright: The Genius and Timeliness of the Traditional Catholic Mass* (2020, Angelico Press).

For more about various aspects of the *Book of Common Prayer* by a range of authors, see *The Book of Common Prayer: Past, Present and Future* edited by Prudence Dailey (2011, Continuum).

For further history of the *Book of Common Prayer*, see *The Rise and Fall of the Incomparable Liturgy* by Bryan D. Spinks (2017, SPCK).

Using the Book of Common Prayer: A Simple Guide by Paul Thomas (2012, Church House Publishing) is an excellent resource for those leading services.

And for a warm and helpful appreciation of Choral Evensong, see *Lighten our Darkness: Discovering and Celebrating Choral Evensong* by Simon Reynolds (2021, Darton, Longman and Todd).

Chapter Five
Living in Community: Patriarchy and Equality

The previous three chapters considered the differences between high-church and low-church approaches to Christianity, the vertical axis which opened up as a result of the Reformation. The final three chapters look at the horizontal axis of my diagram, the scale from conservative to liberal. This measures Christian attitudes to the changes in society which have taken place since the Industrial Revolution. It asks whether those changes are symptoms of a society which is moving away from faith, or whether they result from new opportunities to express Christian values more deeply.

The goal of this chapter will be to explore the debate about whether women can hold positions of leadership in the Church, a subject which divides opinion today. But, to set the scene and to clarify how these discussions work, I will begin by looking back at an earlier social change which is no longer controversial.

HOW WE INTERPRET THE BIBLE: THE EXAMPLE OF SLAVERY

Imagine that a dodgy-looking man in a white Transit van approaches me in a quiet corner of the supermarket car park one day. And he says: 'Pssst… want to buy some slaves?' Then he opens up the door of his van enough for me to see that there are some healthy-looking captives chained up inside. He explains to me that he is able to offer them today at a very special discount price.

This is not how I am expecting my day to turn out, but I have a think about how useful it would be to have a slave or two to help me. I consider some of the menial tasks I could get them to do. Unfortunately, there is a vague nagging feeling in the back of my mind that the owning of slaves might not be entirely harmonious with my Christian faith or with the ethical life expected of a minister of religion. So I take out my phone, launch my Bible study app, and I do a comprehensive search for all the references to slavery in the Bible.

And, to my relief, it is very good news! Owning slaves turns out to be fine. St Paul tells slaves that they should obey their masters as if they were serving Christ.[105] That sounds like an extremely promising work ethic. Surprisingly, he does not say: 'Slaves, run away! God will help you escape.' He does place some limitations on the conduct of slave-owners by saying that they should treat their slaves justly and fairly,[106] but I think I could probably manage to do that. And, best of all, he does not say, 'Slavery is bad, let your slaves go immediately!'

The most obvious, literal, straight-forward reading of Holy Scripture by someone seeking to be faithful and obedient to God's command-ments therefore tells me that slavery is absolutely fine. This means that I can go ahead with my purchase, and may never again need to clean the chicken coop, scrub the toilet or empty the bins.

Surprising though that view may sound to us today, this was not an unusual opinion in the past. For most of our history, Christians shared with other faiths and cultures the assumption that slavery was just part of the way that the world inevitably worked. They held that assumption in the same sort of way that we today accept that there will be people cleaning offices who earn the minimum wage. It is simply the way things are. Before democracy spread in the modern world, slav-ery seemed to be part of the unavoidable inequalities and established power dynamics of human society. There were popes and other clergy who owned slaves, while feeling fully entitled to hold their heads up high as respectable Christian gentlemen. The greatest names among Catholic and Protestant theologians said that slavery was acceptable, including Augustine, Aquinas, Luther and Calvin.

---

105   Ephesians 6.5
106   Colossians 4.1

Slavery results from poverty and from human conflict, both of which are found throughout history. Today we think that wars conclude with very civilised discussions followed by handshakes and signatures and the resumption of normal life. But, for most of history it was normal for victors to slaughter or to enslave their defeated enemies, having plundered their settlements. The options open to those conquered in battle would often just be slavery or death. The Roman Empire enslaved many, as did the Vikings when they frequently raided England. Christians and Muslims took away each other's liberty during clashes in the Middle Ages. And slavery was widespread within Africa, even before it was further encouraged by Arab slave traders and then by the notorious Atlantic slave trade run by Catholics and Protestants, including many English merchants. None of this approval of slavery is unusual: every other part of the world has its examples.

Even for those who were not slaves, life in pre-industrial societies did not include much that we would today recognise as freedom. The average medieval peasant would have no real option other than to work on the land and to pay rent to the local landowner. They would have had very few of the opportunities open to us, and certainly no voice at all in local or national government.

The abolition of slavery is therefore not the removal of an isolated evil anomaly, but is a key part of the development of human society towards a greater valuing of freedom and human rights. As I suggested in Chapter Two, the growth of a belief in democracy and liberty is deeply interwoven with the history of Protestantism and the development of Evangelicalism, which teaches that all should be able to read the Bible for themselves and to make their own decisions about whether or not to follow Jesus Christ. Protestant societies also led the way in gaining new prosperity from industrialisation and from increased trade, in which the influential new 19th-century middle classes were comprised substantially of Evangelicals. And, as I mentioned in Chapter Two, it was Evangelical Christians who led the way in getting the slave trade abolished in the 19th-century British Empire, which was then the world's greatest trading superpower. The most famous of the campaigners was William Wilberforce, an independent Member of Parliament who spent most of his life campaigning against slavery after his Evangelical conversion.

The abolition of slavery therefore provides a very interesting example of how the Bible actually works and how Christians take part in social changes. On the face of it, the Bible is completely fine with slavery. And yet, some of the people who believed strongly in the supreme authority of scripture were the ones who led the way in campaigning for the release of slaves. Today's view of slavery did not arise from people abandoning the Bible because they had found a better guide to ethics, it arose from them looking more closely into its deeper meaning.

So why did those Evangelical Christians campaign against slavery? Their way of taking the Bible very seriously did not just treat it as a list of rules which were fixed for all time. They realised that there were ideals and values within it which did not fit well with slavery. They realised that the Bible, read as a whole, held more significant truths which went beyond a superficial reading of those few verses about slavery.

In the Bible, Jesus said that we should love those around us as much as we love ourselves.[107] St Paul said that Christ has come to bring reconciliation between people and God, and to break down divisions between different groups of people.[108] He said that, in Christ, there is no longer Jew or Greek, no longer slave or free, no longer male or female, but that all are one.[109] Jesus talked about the Kingdom of God transforming the world, so that the last would be first and the meek would inherit the earth.[110] And he said that the Spirit of the Lord had anointed him to bring good news to the poor, to proclaim release to the captives, and to let the oppressed go free.[111]

From those central Christian values flows very logically a longing for a better world, an interest in social justice, a desire to break down barriers, and a quest for a society which fairly includes all people rather than victimising any particular groups. History shows us that there is

107   Luke 10.25-37
108   Ephesians 1.11-22
109   Galatians 3.28
110   Matthew 13.31-33
111   Luke 4.18

plenty in the Bible to inspire people to campaign against slavery, even though the obvious verses about slavery mostly seem to be fine with it.

This illustrates how the Bible does not function as a definitive list of laws and detailed instructions, even for Evangelical Christians. It is a lot more dynamic than being a perfect set of rules and regulations for us to follow blindly. Christianity was always supposed to be about life in the Holy Spirit rather than merely obedience to the letter of the Law, as St Paul makes clear.[112]

It seems to me that the Bible shows what happens when the highest of ideals meets the messy realities of human life. God, who is the source of all goodness and truth, comes into relationship with human beings. But those human beings are limited by their own selfishness and by the constraints and compromises of their particular situations. The Bible describes the most highly exalted, beautiful, inspiring, moral ideals: love God; love your neighbour; blessed are the peacemakers; blessed are those who hunger and thirst for righteousness; we are all one in Christ. But then those ideals have to be lived out within the troubled realities of sinful human lives and within all the limitations and compromises of human society. God has to start somewhere, within the limitations of particular contexts.

It is important for us therefore to understand the context of the verses in the Bible which accept slavery. This was a patriarchal society, ruled then by absolute imperial power, which included slavery as an essential part of its structures. The Church, at that time, was a small, persecuted minority group, with no rights, no power, no ability to change its society. If a group of radical Christians had tried to present a petition to the Roman Emperor demanding an end to slavery, they would probably have met with laughter or total bafflement. Trying to get slavery abolished in the first century would not have occurred to them as a serious possibility.

So St Paul does not set out a detailed plan to transform the economic and social structures of his society. That simply was not an option then. Instead, he stays very safely within all of those structures, showing how to live a compassionate Christian life within the rules of the day.

112   2 Corinthians 3.6

He tells slave-owners that they are accountable to God, who shows no partiality, and that they have a duty to treat their slaves justly, fairly and without threatening them.[113]

Here is a summary of Paul's references to the social structures of his time, referring to the obedience required by slaves and by wives.[114]

- Wives are to obey their husbands, as the Church obeys Christ.
- Husbands are to love their wives, as Christ loved the Church and gave his life for it.
- Children are to obey and honour their parents.
- Fathers are to avoid provoking their children, but to bring them up in the discipline and instruction of the Lord.
- Slaves are to obey their masters, as they obey Christ.
- Masters are to stop threatening their slaves, knowing that all have the same Master in heaven.

Paul also writes:

> Let every person be subject to the governing authorities; for there is no authority except from God, and those authorities that exist have been instituted by God. Therefore whoever resists authority resists what God has appointed, and those who resist will incur judgement.[115]

The First Letter of Peter also tells slaves to accept the authority of their masters, and says this:

> For the Lord's sake accept the authority of every human institution, whether of the emperor as supreme, or of governors, as sent by him to punish those who do wrong and to praise those who do right.[116]

These references to 'governing authorities' describe Roman imperial rule, which in today's world would be called a violent dictatorship with an appalling disregard for human rights. It would cause today's democratic countries to shudder disapprovingly and start imposing

113   Ephesians 6.9
114   Ephesians 5.21-6.9
115   Romans 13.1-2
116   1 Peter 2.13-14

sanctions. But the New Testament writers tell Christians to accept this entire set of governing authorities and social structures as they are, concentrating on advising ways in which they can be loving and responsible within those structures.

For most of Christian history, this approach seemed totally unsurprising. Paul's assumptions about the structures of society mapped quite easily onto the hierarchical structures of medieval Catholic Europe. In an ancient or medieval society, everyone knew their place and all were very familiar with their duty to obey the men in charge. The devout Christian hope then was that the governing authorities would impose Christianity on everyone and that all people would seek to use whatever power they had responsibly and compassionately.

Yet Protestants have led the way in moving beyond that kind of social system, for good biblical reasons, as I described in Chapter Two. We no longer see vicious dictatorships as good ways of running countries, nor do we expect monarchs to impose Christianity with threats of death. We think that democracy and liberty are important aspects of a society with Christian values. In Wilberforce's time, Britain was a country with a strong, widely-shared commitment to Christianity, and there were many keen Christians in positions of real power and influence in the government. They realised that they now had an opportunity which Paul would never have dreamed of. They were able to take the values shown in the Bible a stage further in practice, living out Christian ideals in their context in a deeper way. That is how slavery was abolished, and why I still need to clean my own chicken coop.

The abolition of slavery is just one healthy example of Christianity developing and changing. The modern world has brought a number of new questions and opportunities, but it is not at all unusual for there to be issues in the Church which people have to puzzle over for a while. In fact, through history that is the way things have usually been. The story of Christianity has always been one of growth which comes out of wrestling with new situations, dilemmas and challenges. Although I am writing now about adaptations to social changes in the modern world, every era in the Church's history has presented questions which have been answered slowly. Even the selection of the books of the

Bible was a slow process taking several centuries. The doctrines of the Trinity and of the divine and human natures of Christ developed over a long period, with many impassioned debates. Even within the Bible itself, that process of struggling with questions is very much there. Many parts of the New Testament, for example, grapple with the question faced as the Church expanded into different countries: should people who were not Jewish have to accept the Jewish law in order to become Christians.[117] If our own age brings new possibilities and new arguments, this is not a matter for alarm. It is merely how things have always been.

A CONSERVATIVE VIEW OF THE ROLE OF WOMEN

Few Christians are still arguing seriously for the legalisation of slavery or the reimposition of violent dictatorships, but many do remain attached to another aspect of that traditional social framework assumed in the New Testament. The majority of the world's churches still have an official theology which says that women cannot be their leaders. Many of the members of those churches disagree with that policy, and many of those outside find it baffling or offensive, but their male leaders continue to assume that this view of women is a rule which can never be changed.

A conservative Christian view of women simply says that women cannot be allowed to be leaders in the Church now because they have not been allowed to be before. In particular, they were not allowed to be leaders in the time when the New Testament was written. Jesus himself chose only men to be the apostles, even though he had both male and female followers.

Conservative Evangelicals support this view by emphasising Bible verses which talk about the authority of men, such as Paul's words to Timothy: 'I permit no woman to teach or to have authority over a man; she is to keep silent.'[118] Often, they talk about male *headship*.[119]

117   See especially Acts 10, 11, 15, and the main theme of Paul's Letters to the Romans and the Galatians
118   1 Timothy 2.12
119   Ephesians 5.23

Those who take a traditionalist view do still strongly emphasise that men and women are of equal value in the sight of God, but they say that men and women have different callings. They say that men and women have different and complementary roles, and that leadership is a distinctively male role. They say that this difference is part of the way we are created by God, and therefore is not something which we should dare to change.

Some conservative Evangelical churches keep this approach fairly quiet, being aware that it can be off-putting to newcomers. It can take a little while for people to notice the ecclesiastical glass ceiling in these churches that prevents women taking on responsibilities that go beyond teaching children or doing pastoral work with other women. Others, especially in America, rejoice more loudly in seeing themselves as counter-cultural, confidently blaming many contemporary ills and family breakdowns on the loss of a traditional understanding of male and female roles in marriage.

Meanwhile, conservative Catholics have many centuries of tradition to add to this conservative interpretation of the Bible. Catholics emphasise that their bishops, priests and deacons have always been male, and the Vatican sees the ordination of women as something which the Church cannot even discuss. The male hierarchy regenerates itself and hands on its sacramental power in the same changeless way, following on from the male apostles. For conservative Catholics, this is an argument about the crucial theme of the validity of the sacraments as well as the authority of men. For them, any attempt to ordain a woman would be invalid, and therefore any attempt by that women to celebrate the Eucharist would also be invalid, putting the souls of her congregation in peril. For them and for any Catholics who are doubtful about this issue, absolute confidence in the sacraments of the Church can only be found if ordination is reserved for men.

I do not find these conservative arguments conclusive. As I have shown, Christians now accept that the opportunity to abolish slavery has been a good thing, despite the acceptance of it in the New Testament. Christians have mostly lost any enthusiasm for all-powerful unelected dictatorships, despite the acceptance of them in the New

Testament. We all dissent to some degree from the power structures of the ancient world. It seems to me that there is a strong argument for reassessing the assumption of male authority over women which was universal at the time of the New Testament. Patriarchy may be part of the background context to the Christian message, rather than part of the message itself. As with slavery, we need to think deeply about recent social changes and be willing to take a deeper look at the Bible, instead of simply pulling out the obvious verses that I have quoted above or insisting on blind obedience to tradition. So I will look next at some very dramatic shifts in human life in the last two centuries.

WOMEN AND SOCIAL CHANGE

Having a very unusual surname, I am a keen explorer of family history. I have been able to trace my own ancestors back to the 18th century, looking at parish records of baptisms, marriages and funerals. The earliest Eyeonses I can find were farm labourers in Lincolnshire. It was especially surprising and moving to discover how many children they had, and how many of those children then died very early. Women were having ten or more babies, of which only two or three might survive to adulthood. I found records of family baptisms in which successive babies were given the same first name, as they kept on dying. This is a very different experience of life from the one we have today. Feeding babies and coping with repeated pregnancies would have taken up a huge part of most women's time, energy and attention. It was a dangerous activity, and women often died in childbirth. This urgent focus on procreation in order to provide enough survivors to maintain the species is the natural way of life found among wild animals and birds, and for most of human history it was completely normal for human beings also.

For a family in those days, gathering enough food to feed their children through the winter would have challenged most people almost to their limits, and the task of producing the next generation was an incredibly arduous one. That is what women had to give most of their energies to, just in order for the human race to maintain its numbers. In the pre-industrial world, there was a very obvious and unavoidable division of roles between men and women. Women had babies, and did many smaller-scale tasks which were compatible with looking after infants. Men had roles which often relied on their greater physical strength: farming, hunting and fighting in wars. This division of labour supported the assumption that leadership roles and roles of significant public responsibility were the domain of men. As education developed, it seemed much more important at first to educate boys than girls. In a world shaped by physical labour and by wars fought with human muscles, the idea that men and women could be interchangeable was then usually only mentioned in humour.

That traditional division of roles is a very natural consequence of the physical differences between men and women. There is something about it that can still feel instinctively right. It is the default way for human beings to behave and survive, and it was found in ancient societies all over the world. But the world has changed almost beyond recognition since then. The Industrial Revolution brought huge economic growth and much more stable and plentiful food supplies. Steam-powered boats and trains delivered fertilisers and transported crops. Some of the more recent Eyeonses used coal-fuelled trawlers to fish for cod near Iceland, bringing it back to the port of Grimsby, from where it was sent by railway around the whole country. There were huge improvements in sanitation in this period, including the installation of sewers in cities, and there were great advances in medicine.

As a result, it became much more unusual for children to die, and the UK population doubled during the 19th century. That century also saw rising numbers of middle-class people growing wealthy from the new opportunities brought by industrialisation. Middle-class women who had plenty of servants found themselves getting very bored, and so they started to campaign to be allowed to take on the same kinds of professional jobs as men.

The first female English doctor began work in 1865. Girton College, Cambridge was founded for women in 1869. Women were allowed to vote in British elections from 1918, and the first female member of parliament was elected in 1919. The first female magistrate was in 1920, and the first barrister in 1922.

Meanwhile, in the Church, there were female Methodist preachers for a while from 1771. The Church of England admitted its first deaconess in 1862 and its first female Readers in 1917. Then women were ordained as deacons in 1987, as priests in 1994 and as bishops in 2015. The Church of England is now strongly dependent on the ministry of women, as are various other Protestant churches. By contrast, the Roman Catholic Church in the West is struggling to find enough male priests, and often is dependent on the ministry of dwindling numbers of elderly men.

In today's world, mothers now typically want to have about two children, and can be confident that they will almost certainly survive. We live in an overcrowded society, so we are no longer outraged or surprised when some women choose not to have any babies at all. We seem to have more than fulfilled God's commandment in Genesis to be fruitful and multiply and fill the earth. As a result, women who have gifts for leadership are much freer to exercise and develop those gifts. We value their contributions to most professions, and it seems very odd not to do so in the leadership of churches. So it is important to look more deeply at what the Bible has to say about this matter.

WOMEN'S LEADERSHIP IN THE BIBLE AND TODAY

There are in fact some isolated examples of women in leadership in the Bible, arising in some unusual circumstances. In the Old Testament, there is Deborah who ruled over Israel as a judge and prophetess, described in the Book of Judges. And there is Esther, a Jewish woman who became the Queen of Persia and prevented the massacre of the Jews within the Persian empire. Even St Paul's view of women's roles does seem to vary from one situation to another: he does not always tell them to keep quiet. He allows women to prophesy in the Corinthian church,[120] which means proclaiming to the congregation what they believe God is saying.

He also speaks positively of a female deacon:

---

120 1 Corinthians 11.5

> I commend to you our sister Phoebe, a deacon of the church
> at Cenchreae, so that you may welcome her in the Lord as is
> fitting for the saints, and help her in whatever she may require
> from you, for she has been a benefactor of many and of myself
> as well.[121]

So there are enough examples of women's leadership in the Bible to suggest that there is nothing inherent in the created nature of women preventing them from ever having authority.

Looking more deeply, there are two very important themes which emerge from Paul's writing. Firstly, he speaks several times about the importance of every member of the Church putting their various gifts to work for the common good, and of everyone valuing each other's contributions. He uses the analogy of a human body in which every organ has a useful role to play.[122] It is a major theme of his teaching, which he argues for in a very straightforward and practical way, without adding any complicated exceptions. He never mentions any category of people who have developed useful skills who should then be banned from using those skills in the Church.

In our context, when women are as likely as men to go to university, and when women are prepared for leadership roles in secular contexts, Paul's logic points towards them contributing those same talents in the Church. I think that his approach suggests for us today that any woman who displays genuine gifts for church leadership should be encouraged to exercise those gifts, and that it would be an obstruction of the work of the Holy Spirit if women were always prevented from doing so.

I am conscious that there are many debates about women in today's world which are currently in the news and which I do not have the capacity to explore adequately here. Different waves of feminism sometimes clash with each other, or may come into conflict with today's focus on the needs of transgender people. There are some campaigns that say women should be treated identically to men and other campaigns that say women need distinctive protections and additional opportunities. Not all of this connects together tidily, and online arguments about

---

121 Romans 16.1-2
122 e.g. 1 Corinthians 12, Ephesians 4.1-16

terminologies and group identities sometimes get very fierce. But the main point I would wish to make is one that I think cuts across most of those debates: it is important to accept all individuals as they really are, to support them with the struggles that they face, and to help them to put the talent and potential that they actually have to good use, regardless of being male or female.

In today's world, we have more freedom than ever before to do that. We do not have to prepare all boys to be warriors and labourers and to prepare all girls to be mothers and housewives in order to avoid extinction. We have much more capacity today to treat each other as unique human beings without forcing anyone into stereotypical moulds. We have more scope than ever before to encourage all people to develop their distinctive talents to the full so that they can use them for the common good in very meaningful and rewarding ways. That goal seems to me to be one of the deepest and most universal principles found the New Testament, and it is just as relevant in today's fast-changing world as it was in the first century.

Alongside Paul's focus on individual talents, he secondly has a strong sense of an overcoming of divisions brought about by Jesus, rather than a reinforcement of them, as I have already quoted in reference to slavery. He wrote:

> There is no longer Jew or Greek, there is no longer slave or free, there is no longer male and female; for all of you are one in Christ Jesus.[123]

Christianity is not actually about the policing of male and female roles, whether that is by religious conservatives or by enthusiasts for new ideas about identity. It is about reconciling all people to God and to each other, overcoming all of our human divisions. It is about bringing together people who are different in lots of glorious and fascinating ways, building relationships of love.

If Paul were raised from the dead here today, I think he would be as amazed as any first-century person to find universities with female scholars, and parliaments with female prime ministers, and

123 Galatians 3.28

hospitals with female doctors. He would no doubt also be amazed to find churches with women in many positions of leadership at all levels. After getting over the culture shock, I think that he would approve of all of those developments. I think he would then be very troubled by any suggestion that women should be banned from using gifts in the Church which they are highly skilled at using elsewhere.

I find it strange when conservative Christians try to apply restrictions to women within churches and families that they would not apply elsewhere. A theological argument against women in church leadership needs to talk about the gifts which God has given us in creation. It seems very bad theology if women are allowed to go to university and to vote and to be lawyers, but are then banned from ever preaching from the Bible or celebrating the Eucharist. It is a very naïve use of verses out of context if we use a couple of New Testament quotes to enforce male authority in the Church and in the family, without thinking about the rest of society.

If conservative Christians would like to argue that patriarchy really is God's plan in creation for the whole of human history, then they should also be arguing against female doctors, female members of parliament, female voters, and female academics. If their argument is that God has created men and women to occupy completely separate roles, then they should be talking about the whole of life, not just the Church. Yet very few conservative churches are that consistent: they welcome female students without telling them to abandon their degrees or to ignore elections. It seems odd to me when they try to make Christian ministry a museum commemorating a patriarchal world which has long since otherwise been passing away.

The first Christians were amazed to find that people who were not Jewish were also receiving the Holy Spirit, and had to rethink their understanding of the boundaries of God's activity. I think that many people have been in a similar situation over the last century when they have experienced the ministry of women in the Church. They have seen, perhaps to their surprise, that God really is doing through women what they may have thought he only did through men. The experiences of those women are significant: female clergy speak of their sense of being called by the Holy Spirit in the same ways that male clergy do. And others experience their ministry in the same ways as the ministry of men. I have been greatly impressed and blessed by the work of the ordained women I have known. Indeed the Eucharist, which seems to me to make God's presence so tangible, has in my experience the same effect when a woman presides at it, regardless of any conservative Catholic anxieties about its validity.

For all of these reasons, I myself am delighted that all roles in the Church of England are now open to women. And I hope that the Church can now be in a stronger position to support those seeking equality for women in all areas of society. In the daily news, there are debates about inequalities of pay between men and women, glass ceilings in various professions, online bullying, domestic violence, the low conviction rate for rape, and the everyday harassment of women. The love of God revealed by Jesus Christ should prompt us to care about those issues as much as William Wilberforce cared about slavery.

THE CENTRE?

Conservative Christians may at this point wish to complain that I have simply taken the liberal side of the argument, and that there is nothing remotely moderate about my position. Nevertheless, I do still feel that there are large groups on both sides of me, and that they are going wrong by heading in their opposite directions.

On one side are those conservatives who think that they can quote a few Bible verses out of context and arrive at a ban on women's leadership in the Church. They fail to look more deeply at how we actually use the Bible across a range of issues, they ignore historical context, and they do not look at the genuine leadership gifts which women display in other areas of modern life. On the other side, are those liberals who think that there is no point in paying any attention to the Bible on this sort of issue any more. They assume it is simply outdated and wrong, and leave it unread.

I find both of those groups disappointing. But they alarm each other even more, each inspiring the other side to become more extreme. Conservatives of that kind proclaim their verses out of context, causing the liberals to conclude that all this stuff belongs in the Stone Age. And liberals of that kind take their lead from secular Western culture rather than from reflecting deeply on the Scriptures, causing the conservatives to conclude that they are not actually Christian.

People who are pushed to either of those extremes seem to me to have missed an important opportunity. A better approach is to look more seriously at the Bible and the ways in which its deepest themes guide the Church, while learning how to connect its message to the world we live in today. That is harder work than either ignoring the Scriptures or turning a few verses into slogans, but it is the worthwhile task which I have been seeking to outline in this chapter. I will continue with that kind of task in the next chapter.

SUGGESTIONS FOR FURTHER READING

A diverse group of authors within the Church of England supporting the ordination of women have produced this very helpful little book: *Women and Men in Scripture and the Church* edited by Steven Croft and Paula Gooder (2013, Canterbury Press).

For the conservative Evangelical arguments against women's leadership, see *Recovering Biblical Manhood and Womanhood: A Response to Evangelical Feminism* edited by John Piper and Wayne Grudem (2006, Crossway).

Chapter Six
Sexuality: Parenthood and Authenticity

INTRODUCTION

This chapter will look at the subject which has been most energetically debated in recent years: Christian understandings of sexuality, including same-sex relationships. As with slavery, violent dictatorships and the roles of women, I want to suggest that taking the Bible seriously does not mean pulling a few verses out of context and assuming that they contain God's complete answer for all time. I have shown that we do not use the Bible that way in relation to other issues, and I am going to argue that we should not use it that way in relation to homosexuality. Instead, we need to look more closely at what the Bible really says, being attentive to the ways it actually works. We need to search for the deeper themes in Christian views of people and relationships and think about how they apply to our situation today.

First, it is worth noting again the contrast between today's world and the world in which the Bible was written, especially due to the changes of recent decades. The culture of today's Western world includes an emphasis on sexual freedom on a scale which is unprecedented in human history. Sixty years ago, a man and a woman who lived together without being married would be described as 'living in sin'. They would be the centre of much local gossip, and a source of great embarrassment to their more respectable relatives. Sixty years ago, two men in a sexual relationship would be committing a criminal offence which carried a prison sentence.

There is now a much greater openness about sex, both in the options that are legally and socially acceptable and in the issues that we talk about. That openness, I think, is bringing a much greater awareness of what can be good about human sexuality and what can be bad about it.

On the good side, there is a greater awareness that sex seems to be a healthy dimension of human activity in a wider range of circumstances, including in some relationships which our ancestors would have found unconventional or immoral. There are people enjoying very healthy relationships and very positive expressions of human sexuality which were previously prohibited by traditional societies.

On the bad side, there is also a much greater awareness of sexual behaviour which is devastatingly harmful. We are more aware than before of the widespread occurrence of the sexual abuse of children. We are more conscious of a whole range of selfish and predatory behaviour, from harassment to rape, so that issues of consent and sexual violence are being discussed more than before. The #metoo movement has high-lighted the degree to which women face sexual assault and harassment even while simply trying to build a career or use public transport. It is now clearer that the great sexual liberation which opened up in the 1960s and 70s has encouraged many men to objectify women with an attitude that often lacks basic respect, let alone love.

Sex is quite literally a matter of life and death. It can create new life and it can enhance loving relationships. But it can also spread deadly diseases or cause the kinds of emotional devastation which people are still talking to therapists about decades later. It can be part of the most powerful and life-affirming experiences of intimacy, as a deep expression of love, vulnerability and trust; or it can be part of the selfish and destructive use of others for shallow, fleeting pleasures. There is much that is very good, much that is very bad, and there are a great many ambiguous and puzzling grey areas in between. When survey-ing this complex landscape, it is easier to go to the extremes of being highly disapproving or wildly permissive than it is to look for a wise way through the complications. The Church has usually erred on the cautious and disapproving side, often very strictly.

THE TRADITIONAL CHRISTIAN VIEW OF SEXUALITY

Christianity affirms the goodness of sex within heterosexual marriage, seeing that goodness as being primarily about the birth of children within a stable home. It also affirms the goodness of celibacy in allowing individuals to have a single-minded devotion to God. Meanwhile, it has traditionally been very stern in opposition to all other expressions of human sexuality.

That traditional Christian view of sex regarded absolutely everything other than total celibacy or the making of babies by married couples as falling short of God's plan and therefore sinful. It worried that any other experience of sexual pleasure (whether alone or with others) was selfish, degrading and destructive. It worried that anything other than heterosexual marriage or celibacy involved being enslaved by irrational passions. And it worried that anything else would be comprised of addictive behaviour, distracting us from our true calling to love God and to love each other. Celibacy or procreation were the only acceptable options, and contraception was seen as a perversion of nature.

Through much of Christian history, Christian legislators were especially concerned about men having sex with men, regarding it as an abomination which was highly corrupting to young men and boys. In comparison, lesbianism seemed far less threatening and went largely unnoticed. But anal sex was punishable by death in the United Kingdom until 1861, and by imprisonment from then until 1967, in a sincere attempt to purify society from something perceived as a great evil. For most of the history of the Church, the death penalty was understood to be the authentic Christian response to gay sex, on the basis of a verse from the Old Testament book of Leviticus, which I shall discuss later.[124]

Even the most conservative of Christians have been moving away from one or more aspects of the very harsh and fearful approaches I have just described. Use of contraceptives is now officially accepted by Protestants and unofficially by most Catholic lay-people, and Christians rarely argue for the return of the death penalty for a consensual sexual act. Those who now argue for the traditional biblical condemnation

124 Leviticus 20.13

of homosexuality are usually unaware that that this would actually involve executions. Instead, they merely say that Christians should repent if they have pursued a gay lifestyle, failing to note that they have an updated interpretation of scripture which has only been found in a brief window of recent history.

Meanwhile, it has become more obvious that the cautious approach of restricting sex to heterosexual marriage does not prevent all problems. We have become more aware of domestic violence within some of those marriages. And the last few decades have uncovered the huge scandal of child abuse by priests who have failed to bury their sexual desires beneath vows of celibacy. There is evil to be found even inside the Church's very cautious traditional boundary. At the same time, we are increasingly aware of the goodness which can exist outside that boundary, including those same-sex relationships which are genuinely loving and which cause those involved to flourish in an atmosphere of real kindness.

We are surrounded by good and evil in human relationships, and the Church should help people to embrace the good and to reject the evil. It should help people to navigate through those grey areas, offering the wisdom and experience of the ages to those who make poor choices when in the grip of temporary infatuations. Increasingly, the traditional Christian rules seem to be too simplistic, but they are developing. The understandings of sex held by Christians have already evolved more over the last century than most people have realised.

I shall now take a more detailed look at the history of the Jewish and Christian understandings of sexuality, from the Old Testament to the present day.

SEX AND THE BIBLE

A great many conservative Evangelicals like to think that they are bravely holding to the one authentic Christian understanding of sexuality established for all time. Sadly, this tends to involve pulling a few Bible verses out of context and assuming that the interpretation attached to them by their particular church in the last few decades is the only one which a true Christian could ever have believed.

Yet the Bible itself is much more surprising and needs to be looked at much more carefully. It does not even require monogamy: men are allowed as many wives as they like. Nor, as I have already described in Chapter Three, does it ever suggest that religious wedding ceremonies are part of what the Church is meant to do, so it never explicitly addresses the question of sex before marriage.

However, it does say a lot about children and a lot about love. The Bible as a whole presents the vast story of the love of God: a love that multiplies itself, overflowing in the creation of the universe, bringing people into existence. This love brings salvation, reconciling people to God and to each other, inspiring people to grow as those who love. That narrative of creation and redemption is the Biblical context for all Christian theology, and it must be the context for our understanding of human sexuality. Indeed, we find that the theme of creation is dominant in how sex is described in the Bible. This must surely be the first and most significant thing to say about human sexuality: sex is the means by which people are made.

THE OLD TESTAMENT

The first commandment from God to the human race reported in the Bible occurs in Genesis chapter 1. It is to 'be fruitful and multiply and fill the earth.' God creates human beings and tells them to create more human beings. The commandment to multiply is at the heart of how human sexuality is described in the Old Testament, with perhaps some surprising consequences. The Bible does not start from the kind of straightforward emphasis on monogamous happy couples that many people like to think it does.

Later in Genesis, God promises Abraham that his descendants will be more in number than the stars in the sky. Abraham's way of living up to this role involves having children both with his wife Sarah and with her slave-girl Hagar.[125] His grandson Jacob becomes the father of the twelve tribes of Israel by marrying two sisters and by also having sex with their maidservants.[126] This is the kind of approach to religion

125 Genesis 15.5 and chapters 16 and 21
126 Genesis 29, 30, 35

that tabloid journalists appreciate immensely. Among those descendants is the greatest King of Israel, King David, who has eight wives
and a number of concubines.[127] Then his son and heir Solomon seems
to be the record-holder, with seven hundred wives and three hundred
concubines.[128]

Behind all this polygamy was the urgent sense that human sexuality was all about building big families. It was about building a strong
nation by having as many children as possible. In an under-populated
world with a low life expectancy, there was an urgent need for more
offspring. At times when many men died in battles, it made sense for
those men who survived to have multiple wives, in order to produce
more young fighters as efficiently as possible. Psalm 127 says: 'Like
arrows in the hand of a warrior are the sons of one's youth. Happy is
the man who has his quiver full of them.'

The Old Testament therefore largely accepts polygamy without comment, and in some circumstances it actually commands it. There is a
law which says that when a married man dies without leaving a son,
his brother must marry the widow, without mention of any exemption
if the brother is already married.[129] The intention is that they can then
have a son who will take the name of the deceased man. The continuation of life through one's earthly descendants is very important in
the Old Testament, which only in its final stages arrives at a belief in
life after death.

Genesis contains a very significant example of someone who fool-
ishly tries to avoid this approach.[130] Onan is given the task of getting
his dead brother's wife pregnant in order to raise up offspring on his
behalf. But he resents the fact that the children will be regarded as his
brother's, and so attempts a basic method of contraception. As it del-
icately says in Genesis, 'whenever Onan went in to his brother's wife,
he spilled his semen on the ground.' It goes on to say that this practice
was displeasing in the sight of God, and that the Lord put him death
as a result. All of this demonstrates, I think, that the main principle at

127   1 and 2 Samuel
128   1 Kings 11.3
129   Deuteronomy 25.5-10
130   Genesis 38.6-10

work in the Old Testament's understanding of sexuality is the urgent need to strengthen the tribes of Israel by having big families and producing lots of children.

That, I think, should be seen as the context for that famous condemnation of homosexuality which occurs twice in the Book of Leviticus. It declares that for a man to have sex with a man is an abomination, and instructs that the offenders be put to death.[131]

I do think it is important to ask what is being condemned in Leviticus and why. Christians are usually very content to try to understand the other laws in Leviticus as rules which relate to a particular context, rather than as God's will for all time. Lots of things are condemned as abominations in Leviticus, including various menu options and the eating of leftovers two days after a sacrifice.[132] We do not follow all the dietary regulations any more, or the ban on making clothes out of more than one fibre (like the polyester-cotton shirt I am wearing).[133]

We can find out some more about the ancient Jewish attitude to homosexuality from Philo (c. 20 BC – 50 AD), a first-century Jewish theologian. He said that the fundamental problem with any man pursuing a sexual relationship with another man was that he would not produce any children. Philo wrote:

> He pursues that pleasure which is contrary to nature, and since, as far as depends upon him, he would make the cities desolate, and void, and empty of all inhabitants, wasting his power of propagating his species… Like a worthless farmer, he allows fertile and productive lands to lie fallow, contriving that they shall continue barren, and labours night and day at cultivating that soil from which he never expects any produce.[134]

Using the same logic, Philo also objected to any man marrying a woman who was known to be infertile. Same-sex relationships offended against ancient Israel's understanding of sexuality because they could never lead to babies. But, perhaps uniquely in the human response to

131 Leviticus 20.13, 18.22
132 Leviticus 7.18
133 Leviticus 19.19
134 The Special Laws III.VII (39) translated in C. D. Yonge (1993) *The Works of Philo* Hendrickson

moral laws, I think we have been very thorough in our obedience to the divine command to be fruitful and multiply and fill the earth. That command was recorded when the world's population was in the millions rather than the billions. Now that we have filled the world with 7 billion people who are placing a vast burden on its natural resources, the moral imperative to reproduce is not quite so relevant. All of us think about sex today in a very different way from those polygamous patriarchs in the Old Testament. Those verses from Leviticus do not have the same significance for us.

I should also mention the other notorious passage in the Old Testament relating to homosexuality. This is the story of God's destruction of Sodom and Gomorrah in Genesis 19. This is a very distressing scene which begins with the attempted gang rape of male visitors by male residents. It describes a situation which no moral person would defend, giving a chilling account of an episode of deep depravity. The passage rightly presents sexual violence as abhorrent, but it gives no consideration to the possibility of loving, consensual relationships between men.

One other theme about marriage and children in the Old Testament has been very influential. Alongside their emphasis on procreation, the Hebrew Scriptures emphasise stable family relationships, condemning adultery and prostitution. The second creation story in Genesis 2 portrays Eve as being created from one of Adam's ribs, and says that this is why a husband and wife become one flesh, completing each other. It suggests that a sexual partnership carries a deep meaning and is meant to involve a strong bond, a faithful union of husband and wife. The relationship between husband and wife is then used in several places in the Old Testament as a metaphor for the relationship between God and the people of Israel. This is a very important theme with a lasting significance.

THE NEW TESTAMENT

Where the Old Testament talks about parenthood and faithfulness, the New Testament opens up another option: it tells us about the celibacy of both Jesus and St Paul. This was really quite a revolutionary idea in its time. Both Jesus and Paul show in their own examples and in their teachings that singleness can be a Christian calling. They both lived very dangerous lives involving much travelling which were not compatible with bringing up a family. They demonstrated that it could be a valid Christian option to serve God without marrying and having children.

Paul wrote to the Corinthians that married people may find that their interests are divided,[135] with a conflict between their desire to serve God and their desire to please their spouse. It is a passage which gives very practical advice. Paul says that someone with very strong passions should marry, but that singleness can have great advantages. Here he is echoing the teachings of Jesus, who indicated that some people would choose to be single for the sake of the kingdom of heaven.[136]

So this opens up other ways in which human life can join in with God's work. Instead of creating more people, some may pour their energies, their time and their emotions into serving God in ways which are not compatible with romantic relationships or parenthood. Some who are called to adventurous works of Christian service realise that the ties and compromises of marriage would get in the way.

I find it interesting to see how pragmatic Paul's approach is. His letter is very reasonable, carefully-argued and practical, describing circumstances which all could recognise. He rejects the two extremes of seeing sex as inherently bad[137] or of throwing away all the rules.[138] He would prefer it if lots of people were content to remain unattached and celibate but, if that does not seem to work for them, then he says it is good for them to marry. In none of this does he introduce some mysterious set of instructions sent from on high which are at odds with common sense and ordinary experience. He justifies and explains everything clearly. He is, as I mentioned in Chapter Three,[139] the Bible's great anti-legalist, an advocate of faith and of the life of the Spirit, rather than of obedience to a detailed set of odd regulations. But those who pull verses out of context tend especially to distort Paul, turning him into a bringer of baffling, harsh and troublesome rules.

135 1 Corinthians 7
136 Matthew 19.11-12
137 1 Corinthians 7.1
138 1 Corinthians 5
139 p. 80

In particular, many people today see him as the New Testament's great opponent of same-sex relationships. They regard him as a stern rule-giver who would look at two Christian men in a loving and equal partnership and tell them that, however much they seemed to be flourishing in a life of prayerful companionship, they were breaking God's law. However, it seems to me that the very positive same-sex marriages which have become evident to us today are a situation which Paul had never considered. I cannot find anywhere in the Bible which actually discusses and dismisses the possibility of two people of the same sex committing themselves to a loving, equal partnership. What is conspicuously absent is a paragraph that reads something like this:

> Now, concerning same-sex marriage, I do not wish you to be ignorant. For I have heard that there are two men among you, accepted as your brothers in Christ, who live as if they were husband and wife. They present the appearance of holiness, goodness and mutual love, contributing generously to the work of the Church. Nevertheless, we must obey God, whose understanding is far beyond ours. He has revealed to me the surprising truth that he hates such relationships. So you must warn those men to separate and to be celibate, or God will judge them harshly. If they remain together, you must cast them out from the fellowship of believers.

Paul never said anything remotely like that, even though many people assume that he did. However, the three places where the New Testament mentions sex between men are in Paul's letters, where they occur with little or no explanation. Paul clearly assumes that he is talking about something which is self-evidently degrading, presumably which is observed to be chaotic and destructive, motivated entirely by lust. He therefore gives two brief mentions of homosexual practice in lists of sins: men who have anal sex with men are put into the same category as liars, perjurers, murderers, idolators, adulterers, the sexually immoral, thieves, the greedy and drunkards.[140] These passages say nothing to explain that view, which he assumes is obvious.

140 1 Corinthians 6.9-10, 1 Timothy 1.10

There is some more detail about this perspective in the opening chapter of Paul's Letter to the Romans, where he uses this accepted Jewish view of homosexuality within one of his main arguments. However, even there he is primarily talking about something else, in a letter which tackles the controversial relationship between the Jewish followers of Jesus and the Gentile converts from other nations. Paul's main theme is his insistence that the Gentiles do not need to follow the Jewish law, so he begins the letter by describing an awareness of morality and sinfulness which can be experienced by anyone. His argument is that all people have sinned and are in need of the grace and forgiveness available through faith in Jesus Christ, whether they are Jews or Gentiles.

Paul asserts that God's presence is visible through creation, and he describes a moral order within that creation in which the rejection of God leads to disaster. When people ignore God's ways, God abandons them to the consequences of their poor choices.[141] This is where the reference to homosexuality comes in. Paul writes:

> Men, giving up natural intercourse with women, were
> consumed with passion for one another. Men committed
> shameless acts with other men and received in their own
> persons the due penalty for their error.[142]

So what is that passage really talking about? Those men have already received in themselves the due penalty for their error, says Paul: they have done something wrong and have already suffered its bad consequences. Paul is arguing that God does not need to intervene to reveal his wrath, he merely abandons people to the unnatural and disastrous chaos that their wrongdoings have created.

It is important to realise that Paul's example only works if there are indeed some evident bad consequences. It works if he is describing someone leading a life of lust-fuelled promiscuity, stumbling miserably from one empty hit of pleasure to the next without ever growing in love. It works if he is describing someone who spends all his money

141 Romans 1.18-25
142 Romans 1.26-27

on prostitutes and descends into a pit of debt, shame and self-loathing. It works if he is describing someone who is putting his health at risk and getting into dangerous situations with criminals. But his example fails completely if he is describing a couple who are flourishing within a loving, committed, faithful same-sex relationship, helping each other to grow in patience, compassion and generosity. His example fails completely if he is describing a couple who are supporting each other through all the challenges of life, a relationship which brings overwhelmingly positive consequences. Paul cannot be thinking of relationships like that, as they would not provide a suitable illustration of God abandoning people to the bad consequences of their bad choices.

Sadly, many conservative Christians pull a verse or two out of context and completely reverse Paul's logic. They claim to have found there a rule specially revealed by God about homosexuality which we must obey even if there does not seem to be any point to it. That is the exact opposite of what Paul is actually doing. He is declaring that a divine moral order is part of the way that creation works, and that it can be observed by anyone. He believes that abandoning God's ways leads noticeably to chaos and disaster, a situation which can be obvious to all people whether or not they have the benefit of the laws specially revealed by God to the Jews. He is arguing for something based on rationality and observation, not on a baffling instruction that makes no sense.

Paul does not raise the question of same-sex relationships of love, nor does he say that God has some hidden reason for banning relationships that help people to thrive. His main theme in Romans is that knowing God is *not* about following a set of rules that are mysterious. Jews and Gentiles are in the same position before God because our relationship with him does not depend on a set of surprising rules revealed to a religious minority. So is Paul really condemning same-sex couples who are flourishing in long-term loving relationships, and whose love for each other is faithful and generous? I suspect that he had never met any such couples and had never even considered the possibility that they might ever exist.

At the time of the New Testament, there were things going on in Gentile cities which the Jews were rightly appalled about. Greek culture, for example, approved of sexual relationships between men and adolescent boys, which we would today recognise as child abuse. Wealthy men, who would otherwise have sex with women, penetrated the bodies of male slaves and prostitutes as a casual and easy way of obtaining physical pleasure, which we today would recognise as an appalling abuse of power. It is easy to find examples in the ancient Greek world of homosexual behaviour which illustrate Paul's argument in Romans 1 precisely: situations in which people treat each other in cruel and degrading ways that undermine human relationships and cause very obvious suffering and moral chaos.

If we try to fit a same-sex couple who are flourishing in a loving relationship into Paul's argument, it does not work. I do not think he could have been imagining such people, and there is no reason why he would have had them in mind. He lived in a society which provided no context within which two men or two women could live openly in a long-term, committed, equal, healthy sexual partnership. Any such couples in first-century Israel would have been keeping their relationships very secret, while living in a desperate state of fear. Most people, like Paul, would therefore have assumed that sexual encounters between men would always be furtive, degrading, shameful and lacking in love. The same was true in our own culture until the 20th century, when changes in the law finally allowed homosexual couples to come out of the shadows and to enjoy the same recognition and support in society as heterosexual couples.

We come back then to the same kind of choice that we had when seeking to interpret what the Bible says about slavery and about women. There are a few verses on the subject. We can pull them out of context and assume that they supply God's final word on the matter. Or we can look more deeply at what is actually going on in the Bible.

Back then, hardly anyone considered the idea of a future world without slavery. Hardly anyone considered the idea of a future world in which women could spend much less of their time having children and could have the kinds of careers that men have. And hardly anyone

in ancient Israel considered the idea that a same-sex relationship could
be something genuinely loving, holy, and life-affirming, or could function positively as a cherished part of the fabric of society. They had not
seen the kinds of relationships which we have begun to see around us
today over the last few decades, as gay couples have become a familiar
and valued part of our world.

If they did not consider those possibilities, are we obliged to maintain the social structures of their society? If they did not address the
questions that we are asking, then then do a few words written while
they were addressing some other topics consist of God's final answer?
It seems obvious to me that they do not. As with other subjects, there
has been more for Christians to think about, pray about and discuss.

THE EARLY HISTORY OF
CHRISTIAN VIEWS OF SEXUALITY

As I suggested at the beginning of this chapter, Christian views on sexuality have changed much more than most Christians realise. Having
looked at the Bible, it is now useful to look at Christian tradition and
to see how the interpretation of the Bible has developed over time.

I mentioned earlier that Jesus and Paul were unusual in presenting celibacy as a positive option, departing from the previous Jewish
emphasis on having lots of children. In the early Church, significant
numbers of Christians followed their example and came to regard celibacy as something very positive and liberating. In the manner that Paul
had argued, their celibacy turned out to be a great gift to the Church,
which benefitted greatly from monasticism. Communities of monks
and nuns became the backbone of the Church, providing an amazingly
strong infrastructure of scholarship, teaching, hospitality, medicine and
care for the poor, all woven into a life of prayer and worship. Monasteries had a huge impact on the history of European civilisation and the
growth of Christianity. The monastic vow of celibacy was extended to
parish clergy during the first millennium, enabling local churches to
run economically without the costs of feeding a priest's family.

That success also brought a negative consequence. To a committed
monk, the ordinary people raising families in the world outside could

seem like a second class of Christian. And to a committed monk, sexual desire was a nuisance, an unwelcome distraction and a pointless temptation. To those whose life required them to resist it, the human libido seemed to be entirely a force of chaos, pulling away from rationality, order and the calm of a life of prayer. This meant that the religious professionals, the scholars and teachers, developed a negative view of all human sexuality. They saw it as something which was an unfortunate necessity for the procreation of children among those second-class Christians, but which was otherwise best ignored.

In doing so, it is significant that they got this view not primarily from the Bible, but from their own experience. This was an exercise of reason in their particular context, inspired partly by ancient Greek philosophy. Medieval Catholicism developed an approach to sexual ethics which again, like the teachings of St Paul, was not claiming to rely on mysterious instructions delivered from above. It was founded on rational argument and the observance of nature, known as *natural law*, based on the idea that God has set up the world so that it functions in consistent ways that we can observe and understand. That emphasis on the observable causes and effects seen in the world has strong echoes of Paul's argument in Romans 1.

Following this approach, their rational conclusion was that the intended function of the human sexual organs was the making of babies, and that the seeking of sexual pleasure in any other context was a breach of the natural order. It is this approach to reason which continues to inform Catholic sexual ethics today in its opposition to contraception and homosexuality. The trouble with the way that the Catholic Church developed natural law is that it focussed on the perspective of celibate monks, while ignoring a vast amount of real human experience from others. There is a lot of data from outside the monastery about the positive value of human sexuality beyond procreation, and this is just as much a part of nature as the experiences of those who choose to be single.

By prioritising the viewpoint of those who were trying to ignore their sexual desires, the Catholic Church developed its famously negative and restrictive understanding of human sexuality. It ended up with the traditional separation between the lifestyles of the religious professionals and everyone else. The keenest Christians became priests, monks and nuns and took vows of celibacy. And it was assumed that everyone else would get on with the traditional task of seeking to produce large families.

FROM THE REFORMATION

As I described in Chapter Three, Martin Luther was not well-suited to this monastic life, and spent much of his time feeling extremely guilty and trying very hard to confess all of his failings. After starting the Reformation, he left his monastery and married a former nun. It was his fervently held view that hardly anyone is actually called to celibacy. Protestants closed down monasteries, allowed clergy to marry, and tried to reduce the divide between the lives of the religious professionals and everyone else.

This left Christianity with the very odd contrast that Catholic priests are obliged to be single, while Protestant clergy have usually been expected to be married and to have perfect families who can set an example to the local community. Many Protestant ministers have struggled with the unrealistic expectation that they should be out working every evening and weekend among their flock while somehow also nurturing households of impressively well-adjusted children. It seems to me that there have been many lonely Catholic priests who would have functioned better if they were married, and some single-minded Protestant ministers who would have been happier if they had been allowed to take St Paul's advice about the value of remaining unmarried. I suspect that a true vocation to celibacy is found among some members of both groups, but only a minority.

Another development in recent centuries, shared by Protestants and Catholics, is the trend for churches to work on behalf of governments in regulating marriage according to very clear rules. Countries have become more organised and have demanded more careful records of births, deaths and marriages, especially to help in taxation, military conscription and law enforcement. In England, for example, the 1753 Marriage Act banned secret weddings in order to reduce bigamy, insisting that all weddings must now take place in churches and be carefully recorded in official registers. Civil weddings were then introduced in 1836 to allow more options under government control. In recent years, official ceremonies of all kinds have been in decline as more couples have simply moved in together. Such cohabitation has usually been seen as a modern phenomenon, but it is in some ways a return to the era before the state and its ecclesiastical functionaries felt entitled to document people's lives so thoroughly.

MODERN ATTITUDES TO CONTRACEPTION

In churches, views of sexuality began to shift rapidly in the 20th century, beginning with a dramatic change in Protestant attitudes to contraception. For the first 19 centuries of Christian history, contraception was regarded by all churches as something which was very obviously wrong. Trying to enjoy sexual pleasure without the duty of bringing up children seemed too much like Onan spilling his seed on the ground. It was clearly something very unholy, irresponsible and selfishly hedonistic. All churches agreed that any people who were having sex and trying to avoid making babies were obviously acting against God and offending against the order of nature. They were indulging their own meaningless lusts and descending into moral chaos.

Yet, as I described in Chapter Five, infant mortality rates plummeted during the 19th century and life expectancy soared. By the 20th century, people were starting to think that having big families was no longer quite as urgent and moral as it had been. As more babies survived, there was a more obvious ethical duty to plan families carefully, making sure that parents did not have more children than they were able to look after well. Today we are also more aware of the unsustainable burden placed by our vast population on our planet's resources.

Contraception gradually stopped seeming so hedonistic and scandalous, and began to be discussed more and more openly by respectable Christians. It is possible to track the changes in attitudes among Anglicans through a series of discussions held at successive Lambeth Conferences, meetings of all the Anglican bishops from around the world which are held usually every ten years.

In 1920, the bishops were still worried that artificial contraception would lead to grave moral dangers. They condemned what they called the 'deliberate cultivation of sexual union as an end in itself'. They upheld two principles: the procreation of children was the primary purpose of marriage, and the only legitimate way of avoiding pregnancy was by abstaining from sex.

However, a lot of ordinary Christians were thinking differently by then and, ten years later, the Anglican bishops started to agree. In 1930, they made the revolutionary pronouncement that 'intercourse between husband and wife as the consummation of marriage has a value of its own within that sacrament,[143] and that thereby married love is enhanced and its character strengthened.' They reaffirmed that the primary purpose of marriage is the procreation of children, but accepted the use of artificial contraception in limiting or even avoiding parenthood. That was a revolutionary development in Christian thinking, affirming that sex as a way of strengthening the bond between husband and wife could be a good thing in itself, even if artificial techniques were being used to avoid pregnancy.

Other Protestant churches changed their teachings similarly at about the same time, so that this revolutionary idea is now almost universal among Protestants. Protestant ministers, youth leaders and student workers now consider it normal to enthuse about the goodness of sex within marriage without even mentioning the procreation of children. Instead, much is now made of the idea that sex is meant to bond a man and a woman very closely together, quoting the Genesis 2 theme about the two becoming one flesh. Sex is therefore now understood by Protestants to be something that belongs within marriage because it is meant to be associated with love, trust, genuine intimacy, and as part of the ways in which the couple share their whole selves, body and mind. The procreation of children is now commonly seen as something secondary and optional which may happen later if so desired.

---

143 Anglo-Catholicism was at the height of its influence around 1930, hence this very rare official Anglican reference to marriage as a sacrament, contrary to the Protestant approach I described in Chapter Three.

Most Protestants have forgotten that this view is a very recent development in our history, and one which would have seemed scandalous to most of our ancestors. However, it is common for Protestants to read the Bible as if this is what everyone always thought it meant, failing to understand that Christian teachings about sexuality have developed through time.

Many people were expecting the Roman Catholic Church to update its teachings in the same way, but it is constrained by that troublesome belief in its own infallibility. In 1968, Pope Paul VI amazed the world by reaffirming the traditional ban on contraception in his encyclical *Humanae Vitae*. The official view of the Roman Catholic Church therefore remains the one which had been held by all Christians for many centuries, stating that artificial contraception is inherently evil. The only valid sexual activity for Catholics is sexual intercourse between a married man and woman who are not using artificial measures to prevent pregnancy.

However, it would seem that most ordinary Catholics are not paying attention to the words of the celibate old men in the Vatican. The size of Catholic families has been shrinking, first in the West and then increasingly around the world. The birth rate in Italy is currently 1.4 children per woman. Overwhelmingly, Catholics share with Protestants the perception that sex can be something which is good in itself within a loving and committed relationship, helping to bond a couple together in a very intimate way.

RECENT DEBATES ABOUT HOMOSEXUALITY

Helped by this separation between sexuality and procreation, the discussion has logically moved on to same-sex relationships. At the same time that the Vatican was preparing its report on contraception, the debate over homosexuality was gathering pace. Parliament voted in 1967 to decriminalise homosexual acts in private between men over the age of 21 in England and Wales, and then equalised the age of consent at 16 in 2001. In the UK, the Lesbian and Gay Christian Movement was founded in 1976, as enthusiasm grew among Christian churches for affirming same-sex relationships. Anecdotal evidence suggests that there always has been an unusually high proportion of gay men among churchgoers, clergy and church musicians, and some of the high-church parts of the Church of England were quietly known to be especially hospitable to them. As their existence became more widely recognised and discussed, many were sympathetic and supportive. But there were also outbursts of opposition in the Church and in wider society, especially during the HIV/AIDS crisis of the 1980s.

Public opinion gradually shifted over the following years, and the UK introduced civil partnerships in 2005 and same-sex marriages in 2014. Some Christians, especially those of older generations, were among the most outspoken opponents of these developments. Few argued for the recriminalisation of homosexuality, merely for the view that the Bible showed it was incompatible with a Christian life. But some churches began to bless same-sex marriages, finding widespread and growing support for doing so, especially among younger Christians. The Church of England seems to be moving slowly and inevitably in that direction, through a long series of discussions and consultations which attempt to balance the views of different groups. The situation is complicated by the fact that some other parts of the Anglican Communion, especially Nigeria and Uganda, are strongly opposed. But some other denominations which are more uniformly liberal are already holding same-sex weddings.

My view is that conservative Protestants and conservative Catholics are both in a rather precarious situation with regard to their teachings about homosexuality. The Catholic Church is officially clinging to the traditional logic which says that sex exists only as nature's way of making babies, which provides a clear and consistent reason for dismissing homosexual relationships without any discussion. This a precarious situation because most of their lay people seem to think that they are wrong about contraception.

Then there is an inconsistency in the current approach of conservative Protestants. They have accepted very enthusiastically that a man and a woman can marry and have sex while carefully avoiding pregnancy, regarding sex in that context as a good thing in itself. So it is odd to refuse to consider that it might also be good for a same-sex couple. Protestants rejoice in the ways that sex can help to join a man and woman together in a lasting, loving relationship, so it is odd not to consider that it might have the same kind of good function in a marriage between two men or two women. The idea that sex without babies can be a good thing but only for heterosexual married couples was the prevailing view of respectable British society for part of the 20th century, a very small slice of Christian history. Some of today's older Christians may look back to that brief era with nostalgia, but it is unconvincing to think that it uniquely represented the one true interpretation of the Bible for all time.

SEX AND THE PURPOSES OF GOD

Having looked through the Bible and the history of the ways it has been interpreted, I will now draw these various themes together to suggest a credible approach for today. A Christian understanding of sex belongs properly within a theological understanding of creation and redemption. The Bible describes how God creates life and then acts to draw people into loving relationships with him and with each other, and the main thing we need to determine is how our human sexuality can be aligned with what God is doing in that work of creation and redemption. Clearly, when a husband and wife bring up children within a loving home, that is aligned with God's creative purpose. Or when celibate priests or missionaries devote their lives to bringing Christ's message of reconciliation to a troubled community, that is aligned with God's redemptive purpose. These two Christian ways of life are well established, but heterosexual marriage or celibacy are not the only two options that could fit into an understanding of creation and redemption.

Now that people are able to live openly in same-sex relationships, there is more and more evidence that those relationships can be very positive indeed. They can be deeply loving, providing a setting within which people nurture each other as faithful Christians. The fruit of the Spirit can grow in those relationships: love, joy, peace, patience, kindness, goodness, gentleness, faithfulness and self-control.[144] Same-sex marriages can enable people to be a support to those around them, and a sign of God's love. All of these qualities seem to be aligned with God's project of bringing healing and reconciliation to the world.

Sadly, the Church's traditional hostility to same-sex relationships does seem to have been getting in the way of that project. Large numbers of people who do not fit the expected heterosexual pattern have felt judged, condemned and excluded from the life of the Church. A lot of people have turned away from a faith in Jesus Christ because it has seemed inevitably to lead to homophobia. This is a very serious failure on the part of the Church. Like the way in which the Church for many centuries endorsed anti-Semitism, it is a barrier to the serious work of reconciliation to which God calls us.

At the same time, it remains the case that there is sexual behaviour in our world which should be opposed because it is cruel and degrading. There are children being abused, and young people being pressured into sex long before they are ready. There are women being forced into prostitution, and a terrifyingly high rate of sexual assault and rape. There are some same-sex relationships that are deeply damaging, just as there are some heterosexual relationships that are deeply damaging. And there are a lot of people whose sexual feelings lead them into actions which are at best a waste of time and at worst are very harmful. Many are addicted to pornography in ways which distort and disrupt their ability to form positive sexual relationships, and many are addicted to the thrill of casual sexual encounters which are lacking genuine love. There is a lot that is deeply wrong with many manifestations of human sexuality.

We find ourselves in a world in which it is easy to go to extremes in our view of sexuality, and hard to find a wise balance. Some recoil from the abuse and cruelty found in the world, retreating to a traditional suspicion of most expressions of human sexuality. Others react against very strict Christian upbringings, resenting the guilt and shame which they were taught to feel about very natural and healthy desires, and wish there were no rules of any kind.

144 Galatians 5.22-23

Nevertheless, there is a wise balance to be found, a vision of human life which joins in with the loving purposes of God. Human sexuality at its best is aligned with God's creative and redemptive purposes. When it is not just an expression of our brief infatuations and selfish desires, human sexuality can lead to lasting relationships which are fundamental to the fabric of society. It helps to join couples together in a bond where they can share great joys and support each other through sorrows, in sickness and in health, for richer and for poorer. It is part of the cement which builds a home environment in which people can grow in love, in patience, in understanding, in forgiveness, in faith and in holiness. Wherever we come across love which is genuine, life-affirming and helps people to grow, it is the joyful responsibility of all Christians to celebrate and nurture that love.

MONEY, SEX AND POWER

Finding that wise balance and that genuine experience of love is often a challenging and confusing process. But a helpful comparison can be made with two other desires which cause complications for moral human beings. In the New Testament there are strong parallels between the portrayals of money, sex and power, themes which heavily preoccupy human beings and which feature in most of the world's novels, films and news headlines. In fiction, evil characters are usually obsessed with one or more of those goals: perhaps greedily swindling their way to vast private fortunes, cheating their way through multiple affairs, or seeking their own fame and glory by cynically manipulating the lives of others. In Christian tradition, such actions are the sins of greed, lust, and pride, well-known for shrinking our souls and causing havoc for those around us.

The Church has responded most dramatically to these spiritual threats with the monastic vows of poverty, chastity and obedience. The ability of some Christians to renounce money, sex and power completely is a powerful inspiration to others, showing that an authentic and rewarding life can be lived without any of them, often with a remarkable sense of true freedom and joy. Nevertheless, it remains the case that most of us are called to lives which involve entangling ourselves with money, sex and power along the way, learning to enjoy using them for good purposes. This challenge requires wisdom, and the development of the virtues of generosity, faithfulness and humility. It involves learning how to make a responsible use of money, sex and power which can avoid the idolatry of enthroning any of them as the central aim of our lives.

Nearly all of us will need to learn to use money responsibly: seeking to earn a living, to budget carefully, to live within our means, to avoid burdening others unnecessarily, to pay our taxes and to share our resources generously with others. In many cases, that task will be a great struggle. It is easy for human beings to conclude that the great key to a good life is therefore the acquisition of more and more money. Yet Jesus insisted: 'No one can serve two masters... you cannot serve God and wealth.'[145] And he warned: 'Take care! Be on your guard against all kinds of greed; for one's life does not consist in the abundance of possessions.'[146] St Paul famously said that 'the love of money is a root of all kinds of evil',[147] exhorting the wealthy to be 'rich in good works, generous, and ready to share'.[148]

For most of us, a responsible life will involve a savings account and a pension fund, but the pursuit of wealth is not in itself the answer to living well. Money needs to serve a higher goal, which it does when it enables people to exchange resources while putting their talents to good use. When the teacher, the farmer, the train-driver and the nurse benefit from each other's work due to a system of salaries and purchases, money is performing a useful function in the building of society. It does that best when people are more interested in their contributions to the common good than they are in their private fortunes. The greatest irony of the love of money is that it is ultimately self-defeating: the greedy miser who is ceaselessly vigilant in maximising his fortune will never enjoy spending any of it, and will never experience the rewards of using it to help others.

145 Matthew 6.24
146 Luke 12.15
147 1 Timothy 6.10
148 1 Timothy 6.18

The love of power has a similarly famous ability to corrupt, and is similarly self-defeating when it becomes an overriding goal. The world's most powerful emperors and dictators have often become ever more paranoid, knowing that they are always very tempting targets for conspirators and rivals, who may knife them in the back at any moment. Positions of great power turn out to be remarkably anxious and precarious. People who spend their lives trying to control others for the benefit of their own egos are generally insecure and miserable. Jesus warned against the lifestyle of tyrannical rulers, and said that true greatness is actually found in being a servant.[149] The truly rewarding life involves making a positive difference in the world, not in accumulating status and power over others.

Nevertheless, most of us will need to learn to use power in our lives. Most of us will look after children or care for our own parents when they are too old to make good decisions on their own. We will have responsibility for the well-being of others, in our families, communities and workplaces. We should neither seek that power for its own sake, nor avoid it, but should learn to enjoy using it wisely. Jesus' parable of the talents indicates that we are meant to develop skills in managing resources and people. The master says: 'Well done, good and trustworthy slave; you have been trustworthy in a few things, I will put you in charge of many things; enter into the joy of your master.'[150] Those who do not seek power for its own sake but who learn to handle responsibility wisely in improving the lives of others will thereby find the true rewards of power.

The responsible use of power and money offers many parallels with a moral and healthy approach to human sexuality. Sex finds its deepest rewards in the creation of new life and in the building of relationships of love, where there is true kindness, warmth, playfulness, humour, affection, trust, understanding, honesty and intimacy. A celebration of those qualities can be found in the Song of Solomon in the Old Testament, which is full of remarkably sensual and sexual imagery. But making sexual pleasure our highest goal becomes, as with power and

149 Matthew 20.25-28
150 Matthew 25.14-30

money, self-defeating, leading only to a self-centred loneliness. Jesus and others in the Bible warn repeatedly against adultery and against sexual immorality (a term which they do not define, but which comes from the Greek word for prostitute, seeming to indicate promiscuity).[151] The deepest intimacy where sex belongs is associated with the love and faithfulness found in a good marriage, where there is genuine mutual delight, trust and understanding. Those who have many brief and shallow sexual encounters with different partners are never experiencing the true intimacy and deep love which should be at the heart of a sexual relationship.

There is another self-defeating way in which many people today treat sex, placing too much weight on it as the core of a relationship and the greatest sign of compatibility. That is an unwise assumption, as the human sex drive is actually one of the most variable things about us, disrupted by factors such as physical and mental health, stress, medication, hormonal changes, pressures of work, tiredness, and above all by sex's own greatest consequence: parenthood. No couple will find that their sexual desires remain equally synchronised throughout their relationship. Good sex requires the security and true understanding found in a lasting relationship, and any deep and lasting relationship requires the willingness to be patient with each another, while continuing to nurture love, affection, understanding, playfulness and intimacy in other ways. Meanwhile, as a high proportion of our novels and TV dramas remind us, those who give up on faithfulness by cheating on their partners cause great misery and disaster for all involved.

So this is the great surprise of sex, money and power: those who seek them above all else find that their search is self-defeating. But those who seek above all to serve God and to live lives of love will often find far deeper experiences along the way of sexual delight, financial trust and a rewarding exercise of responsibility for others, in ways which help them to grow. It is only by realising that sex, money and power are not what matter most that we can truly benefit from them.

Since the 1960s, the tendency for human beings to make an idol of sex has greatly increased, encouraged by a society which is saturated

151 e.g. Matthew 15.19

with sexual imagery, in which those who are not sexually active are seen as inadequate failures, and in which any mobile phone provides easy access to pornography of the most misleading kinds. There is much here which the Church needs to warn against, because it leads to disappointment, cruelty and misery. There are very good reasons for much of the caution shown by conservative Christians in response to these problems. Trying to be cool by going along with all the whims of our culture would be a great failure.

Instead, the Church has the opportunity to celebrate and encourage strong relationships of genuine love, trust, warmth and faithfulness, whatever the sexes of those involved. Marriage ceremonies are one aspect of that support, but it is even more important to provide good pastoral care for couples and families who are facing challenges in their relationships. A close Christian fellowship can also be a lifeline for those who struggle with the challenges of singleness or bereavement. And it can be a source of wisdom and perspective for those who might be drawn into unhealthy and abusive relationships. All of those forms of support work best when the Church is known for being welcoming and generous rather than harsh and judgemental, and they are a task which the whole Christian community can share in.

ABORTION

I will now change to a different topic for the last section of this chapter, exploring the other great controversy in the ethics of sexuality and reproduction. Just as Christian attitudes to contraception have varied, so have Christian attitudes to the termination of pregnancies. And, as with homosexuality, the role of Scripture and Church tradition in the formation of those attitudes is often also misunderstood.

The ethical dilemma over abortion hinges entirely on the question of when a human being becomes a human being. Is a newly-fertilized egg cell immediately a person, or is it a microscopic dot that is just at the beginning of a journey towards becoming a person? Is using the morning after pill a form of murder or is it something less morally problematic than stepping on an ant? People of different faiths and philosophies have a range of views on this subject, but it is widely assumed now that the official Christian belief is that God has told us that life begins at conception. I am not convinced.

If we start with the Bible, the argument turns out to be even flimsier than the one against same-sex relationships. The Bible actually says nothing at all about abortion. It never mentions it, even in passing, despite the fact that other ancient texts refer to it. This is surprising given that the Bible talks about lots of moral issues, including advice on what to do if you find a bird's nest or a donkey that has fallen over.[152] But abortion is not in there at all. Conservative Evangelicals who claim to avoid using human reasoning and to depend entirely on the Scriptures ought at this point to say that God clearly has other priorities, and to get on with the things that are actually commanded in the Bible (like feeding the poor, looking after orphans, spreading the Gospel, or assisting fallen donkeys) rather than campaigning against abortion clinics.

Instead, the conservative Evangelical logic deploys a large amount of human reasoning in order to reach the opposite conclusion. It says that abortion is such an important issue that there must be something about it somewhere in the Bible. There must be something which God intends to be his complete and final judgement on the matter. An exhaustive search of the Scriptures reveals that the nearest possible candidates are some mentions of babies in wombs: David says that God knitted him together in his mother's womb,[153] and Jeremiah says that God appointed him as a prophet before he was born.[154] From here comes the deduction that God ascribes personhood to the foetus, and then a huge imaginative leap to the conclusion that an embryo is a human being from the moment of conception.

Yet that reasoning goes far outside the intentions of those texts, which are about writers looking in awe at God's plans for their own lives rather than exploring medical ethics. It leaps to a conclusion which has no basis in the text. Consider this analogy: suppose I say that an artist painted a picture in her studio. Am I thereby making any

152 Deuteronomy 22.4,6
153 Psalm 139
154 Jeremiah 1.5

judgement about the point at which the picture became a picture? I do not think so. There are some early stages where there are just a few tentative pencil markings on a white canvas, and it looks much more like a blank page than a painting. Then there are some late stages where it is nearly all finished apart from some bits of sky to colour in, and it is clearly a picture which is slightly incomplete. But the statement that the artist painted the picture in her studio really does not imply that it became a picture from the very first moment at which her pencil touched the canvas. A pencil dot could not be called a painting.

If I say that God knitted me together in my mother's womb, I am clearly saying that I was me by the point of birth, but I am not saying anything about my status during the preceding nine months. There were obviously some early stages involving a microscopic blob, and some later stages when I was very much a baby. If anything, saying that there was a process of me being assembled actually suggests that I was not me in the early stages of that process.

So I really do not think that the Bible gives the answer which many Evangelicals (especially in America) now think that it gives. A Protestant *Sola Scriptura*[155] approach to Christianity applied with any consistency would surely suggest that God is not remotely interested in abortion. If he was, he would have mentioned it.

Looking onwards to Christian tradition, we do then find a clearly-stated opposition to abortion in some early Christian texts, such as the *Didache*, but without any claims about personhood beginning at conception. Where we find later writers studying the matter in more depth, they describe a process of becoming human rather than something instantaneous.

The Greek philosopher Aristotle (384–322 BC) wrote extensively on subjects which we would now label as science, and was highly influential among Christian thinkers (as I described in reference to transubstantiation). He noted the significance of the point in the pregnancy when the mother becomes aware of the movement of the child, saying that this was when the embryo begins to resolve into distinct

155 The Scriptures alone, see p. 57

parts.[156] He wrote about three different levels of life which develop during pregnancy, using the term *soul* as a term to describe life. First, the embryo has a *nutritive soul* which is like that of a plant, suggesting a piece of living matter which is able to grow. Then it acquires a *sensitive soul*, like an animal, suggesting that it offers some kind of instinctive response to its environment. And finally it acquires the *rational soul* which is distinctively human, suggesting that it is acquiring a capacity for thought.[157]

This all sounds very reasonable, as it was meant to be, and it found its way into the writing of St Thomas Aquinas (c. 1225-1274), the most influential medieval Catholic theologian. Aquinas's view was that the vegetative soul and then the sensitive soul are developed by the natural power contained within semen, but that the intellectual soul is specially created by God towards the end of the process.[158]

Abortion was condemned by all Christians at that time in the same way as contraception. However, clear distinctions were made between the nature of the offence at different stages of pregnancy. In the ninth century, a guide for priests hearing confessions gave this advice:

> If any woman has voluntarily destroyed her offspring in the womb before 40 days, she should do penance for one year. But if she has killed it after 40 days, she should do penance for three years; if indeed she has destroyed it after it was animated, she should do penance as a murderer.[159]

Such distinctions are widely found throughout most of Christian history. Abortion, on similar grounds to contraception, was opposed. But abortion in the early stages of pregnancy was treated as a much lesser offence than abortion when the foetus was fully formed, which was treated like murder.

It was as recently as the 19th century that the approach of the Roman Catholic Church was greatly tightened up, for a surprising set of loosely-connected reasons which will send my next paragraphs on a large

---

156   History of Animals, Book VII, Chapter 3
157   Generation of Animals, Book II, Chapter 3
158   Summa Theologiae, Prima Pars, Question 118, Article 2
159   Quoted by Zubin Mistry (2015) *Abortion in the Middle Ages* York Medieval Press, p. 152

detour. The 19th century was a time when the Catholic Church was struggling against many threats to its traditional political power and intellectual status in Europe. Piux IX (who reigned from 1848 to 1878) led a hard-line response which restated Catholic doctrines very boldly. It was Pius IX who presided over the First Vatican Council, which established the dogma of papal infallibility. In 1854, he had proclaimed the dogma of the Immaculate Conception of Mary, so that was then considered to have become an infallible pronouncement.

The Immaculate Conception is a widely-misunderstood Catholic teaching. It does not relate to the birth of Jesus, as people often assume, but to Mary's own conception. The dogma says that Mary was conceived in the usual human manner, but that God miraculously preserved her from inheriting the stain of original sin from her parents. This sets Mary apart from all other human beings apart from Jesus, in being free from sin. Beliefs of this kind had been popular for many centuries among Catholics, but it only became a clearly-defined official teaching in 1854. As I described in Chapter Three, I share the Protestant rejection of this unbiblical idea.

I can arrive at the point at last: the dogma is relevant to abortion because it highlights Mary's conception as the key moment in the formation of her nature and identity. Where Aquinas had written that God acted later in the pregnancy to form a rational soul, this doctrine describes God acting at the very beginning of a pregnancy to establish the most important dimension of Mary's spiritual nature.

With this attention focused on the first moment of embryonic life, Pius IX's tidying up of various regulations then included the removal of all ambiguity about different stages of pregnancy. In a proclamation of 1869 clarifying the Church's response to various sins,[160] the Pope treated all abortions as equally grave. They were to lead to automatic and immediate excommunications, so that any repentant offenders would require the intervention of a bishop if they were ever to be accepted back into the Church.

Thereby the Catholic Church has come to treat the termination of a pregnancy at any stage as if it were murder. Earlier centuries included

---

160 The papal bull *Apostolicae Sedis moderationi*

a wide range of views among leading Catholics about the status of a foetus at different stages of pregnancy. But Catholic caution and a desire for absolute clarity on this important issue has led to the view that a fertilised human egg cell is a human being with a human soul right from the moment of conception.

In neither Scripture nor tradition can I see a divinely given insight that the true essence of humanity is fully present when we are only a single cell. As I described in *The Theology of Everything*,[161] human consciousness is an emergent phenomenon, something that arises from the functions of our brains. That distinctive feature of human nature is not there at the very beginning.

To me, the approach of Aquinas seems much more convincing. There is something there in the early days which is a bundle of cells, with no more intelligence than a plant. It develops into a form of life which resembles a tiny animal, having some basic movements and instinctive responses. Then, as the months go by, its identity as a human baby develops more and more clearly.

Within this gradual process of development, there is no tidy line that can be drawn. This is perhaps the most convincing argument for treating conception as the only milestone in the formation of humanity. Everything else does seem more ambiguous and open to challenge. But, to most people's use of reason today, the termination of a pregnancy near its beginning does not seem to be wrong in the way that killing a baby who is ready to be born would be wrong. Even without a clear dividing line, there is a vast difference.

Perhaps the strongest Christian argument for opposing abortion is the duty of Christians to defend the poor, the weak and the vulnerable. An unborn child falls into that category. However, most of the women and girls who seek abortions also fall into that category. Some of them are victims of rape. Many of them are young, lacking in resources, and may be facing the prospect of caring for a child on their own, perhaps abandoning their education or the early stages of a career that they will depend on. Where a woman is not in a good position to love and provide for a child, it seems to me to be a valid moral choice for her

---

161 *The Theology of Everything*, p. 119-124

to end the pregnancy at an early stage. Indeed, I think there are many women who have shown great moral courage in taking such difficult decisions, and who have been unfairly condemned by Christians.

The story of Christianity and abortion has reached a disturbing chapter in recent American history, where it has become one of the main cultural markers defining the gulf between Democrats and Republicans, and therefore one of the most fiercely-contested moral and political issues. The Moral Majority movement, founded in 1979 by Baptist minister Jerry Falwell and others, brought together a surprising new right-wing alliance of Protestant and Catholic voters in support of the Republican Party. They were able to achieve huge political influence by bringing Catholics (who had traditionally voted Democrat) into partnership with Evangelicals. Those Evangelicals had previously paid little attention to abortion, but their enthusiasm for the political power of a shared moral high ground led them to join the Catholics in condemning it as a terrible sin. The Moral Majority played a decisive role in the election of Ronald Reagan as president, and established the expectation that morally conservative religious Americans will vote Republican and that Evangelical Americans will get very angry about abortion. But those American Evangelicals who now confidently pin a total ban on abortion onto the poetry of Psalm 139 have forgotten that abortion was formerly widely accepted by them.

Meanwhile, in the Church of England, there remains little discussion of these issues. Followers of American social media personalities some-times bring these campaigns to the attention of their English friends. A Google search will reveal some statements produced by Church of England committees expressing a general opposition to abortion com-bined with a recognition that it may sometimes be the least bad option. But this is not something that Church of England people tend to cam-paign about, and that seems to me to be a sane and a biblical approach. There is much more which could be said about the arguments of male theologians and politicians, but my conclusion is that abortion in the early stages of pregnancy concerns something happening to a woman's body and should be a decision for her to make thoughtfully and safely.

CONCLUSION

This chapter has explored several thousand years of the history of the Bible and the Church, covering a set of important moral issues, so I will end by looking back briefly over that history.

The journey began with the Old Testament, which strongly prioritised the procreation of children. Polygamy was accepted in order to maximise pregnancies, and in some instances it was commanded. To avoid having children was seen as rebellion against God. This was a rational response to a time when human population levels were small and precarious, when the people of Israel were in great danger of being overwhelmed by the superior numbers of the hostile surrounding tribes and empires.

In the New Testament, Christianity began to look outwards with a message for the whole world. Paul's adventurous international missionary journeys followed the example of Jesus in opening up another rational view of life. A Christian might be more free to serve God if not tied down by the need to please a spouse and to support a family. Singleness began to seem like a good option, at least for some. This New Testament development later made possible the communities of monks and nuns which contributed immeasurably to the spread of Christian civilisation across Europe and beyond. For those who felt strongly that they were not called to celibacy, Paul still recommended marriage. He condemned prostitution and promiscuity, emphasising the way in which husband and wife become one flesh. His rational approach showed how both singleness and marriage could lead to purposeful, stable lives which supported the goal of planting and growing healthy churches.

Many centuries later, the Industrial Revolution caused the infant mortality rate to collapse and the population to rise steeply. It began to seem appropriate to limit the size of families, while still allowing married couples to have sex as a way of strengthening their relationship. Contraception was therefore approved by Protestants during the 20th century on rational grounds. But the 'infallible' Roman Catholic Church remained officially stuck with the rationality of the pre-industrial era, the natural law argument which had tied sex entirely to procreation.

Then as society became more permissive in the 1960s, and as better contraception further reduced the association between sex and babies, homosexuality was decriminalised in the UK and elsewhere in the West. This enabled positive and healthy same-sex relationships to become widely seen and valued for the first time. It became clear that these relationships could be loving and faithful, contributing to the spiritual growth of both partners and to the wellbeing of local churches and communities. Following further prayerful and rational reflection on life as we observe it, many Christians now seek to affirm those relationships, celebrating same-sex marriages.

Two themes in particular have emerged from this journey. The first is that Christian views of sex have not been static, following a fixed set of commandments revealed for all time. Instead, they have developed as they have taken account of changing circumstances. Beliefs held by conservatives are sometimes not as old as they think. The second theme is that Christian views of sex have tended to arise through processes which are rational and thoughtful, linked to prayerful reflection on how life actually works at the time, rather than relying entirely on ancient rules from a different context.

With these two themes, I am most obviously arguing against the conservatives who assume that their views come directly and immutably from the Bible. Many conservative Evangelicals remain stuck with an odd assortment of 20th century values, believing them to be the true interpretation of Scripture for all time. In their approach, contraception is fine but abortion at any stage is not, homosexuality is completely legal but also completely unchristian, and sex is just for straight married couples, even though making babies is now optional. These are simply the rules of an older generation, a passing phase in our history which is anchored neither to a timeless Biblical truth nor to a rational reflection on life as we experience it today.

Yet I am not seeking to follow those liberals who react against the conservatives by abandoning all our traditions and trying to start again from scratch. There is an ongoing process of prayerful and rational reflection which has characterised the best Christian theology through history. It is a process which we can still participate in today, and which leads to clear and distinctive values about faithfulness and love within an understanding of the creative and redemptive purposes of God.

SUGGESTIONS FOR FURTHER READING

For a traditional Catholic view of sex and procreation, see *Love and Responsibility* by John Paul II, writing before his papacy with the name Karol Wojtyla (reprinted 1993, Ignatius Press).

Same Sex Relationships by John Stott, revised by Sean Doherty (2017, The Good Book Company) offers a clear presentation of the conservative Evangelical argument against same sex relationships.

On the affirming side, a very significant little book is *Permanent, Faithful, Stable: Christian Same-Sex Marriage* by Jeffrey John (2012, Darton, Longman and Todd). Further explorations of that perspective are found in *Amazing Love: Theology for Understanding Discipleship, Sexuality and Mission* edited by Andrew Davison (2016, Darton, Longman and Todd).

The latest Church of England project to discuss sexuality is found in *Living in Love & Faith* (Church House Publishing, 2020). It throws many ideas and perspectives in the air, in a brave attempt to get people with entrenched views to see beyond them, and therefore suffers from a lack of a clear argument. But the accounts of individual experiences are very compelling.

A thoughtful and helpful discussion of abortion is offered by Kira Schlesinger: *Pro-Choice and Christian: Reconciling Faith, Politics and Justice* (2017, Westminster John Knox Press).

Chapter Seven
The Church and the World: Proclamation and Pluralism

INTRODUCTION

In this final chapter, I will look at another question which causes great variation between churches today: do Christians have a duty to proclaim the Gospel in words to non-Christians, seeking to convert them?

An enthusiastic commitment to evangelistic proclamation is often one of the most obvious features of the more conservative churches, especially among Protestants. Evangelical churches exhort their congregations to pray for the conversion of their non-Christian friends, relatives, colleagues and neighbours and to invite them along to services and talks. They seek to enlarge the membership of existing churches and to plant new ones. They often support overseas missionaries by praying for them and raising money for them.

Meanwhile, liberal Christians are quite likely to find such proclamation embarrassing, inappropriate or even offensive. They may be much more hesitant to talk about their religious beliefs, perhaps preferring to focus quietly on seeking to live a good life. If liberal Christians think about any kind of public campaigning, they are likely to think first of social justice or caring for the planet, rather than any attempt to recruit new church members.

Once again, this division between conservatives and liberals involves a contrast in response to a development in modern society. For most of European history, it was assumed that there was one religious truth which a society should seek and embrace together. But people in the West are now mostly content to allow a range of faiths and philosophies to coexist, and are more inclined to celebrate cultural diversity as a positive feature of the world and of many local communities. Without a common commitment to one particular faith, the shared life of a nation is now mostly organised on a secular basis. Faiths are often treated with respect, but now seen as primarily a private matter: they are part of the inner life of families and individuals, rather than a matter for public debate. Religious people are sometimes quick to take offence at any criticisms of their beliefs, which they may see as a challenge to their identity and heritage, and non-religious people may get very annoyed if they think they are being preached at. On all sides, most people find it much easier to avoid the subject. And so, in a society where faith is rarely discussed deeply and where diversity of belief is assumed and valued, it is now a very controversial step to proclaim that the Christian Gospel is uniquely true and universally significant.

In this chapter, I will look at the ways in which different Christians approach that situation today. First, I will look in more detail at the historical background to the social change which provides the context for the dilemma.

CHRISTIANITY AND THE WORLD: A BRIEF HISTORY

Christianity is the world's largest religion, and has succeeded far more than any other faith in taking root in a huge variety of different cultures all around the globe. Where other religions tend to be strongly associated with one or more ethnic groups or nations, Christianity has achieved a much more widespread and diverse presence.

This huge expansion demonstrates something central to Christianity: it is a highly successful missionary faith. Jesus' own teachings are the origin of the idea that this faith is meant to be shared with the whole world. He told the apostles to 'go and make disciples of all nations.'[162] And he said that their message would be heard in 'Jerusalem, in all Judea and Samaria, and to the ends of the earth.'[163] This is exactly what has happened.

162 Matthew 28.19
163 Acts 1.8

From its beginnings in the Middle East, Christianity spread quickly to North Africa and to the south and west of Europe, reaching Britain in the time of the Roman Empire. During the Middle Ages, it was strongly established across the whole of Europe, from Portugal to Russia. After the great age of European exploration began in the 15th century, churches were soon founded in many more countries, and then the work of Protestant missionaries and Bible translators greatly accelerated in the 19th century, taking the Gospel around the world.

Today, Christianity has therefore become a global movement rather than a Western phenomenon, and is especially vibrant in many developing countries. Christians are more now numerous in the southern hemisphere in than the northern hemisphere, and the Church of England's active membership is greatly outnumbered by its Anglican cousins in Africa, especially Nigeria. Tens of millions of Christians can be found in countries such as China, India and the Philippines. For the first time, the Pope is someone who comes from South America rather than from Europe, a fact which is much more representative of the distribution of today's Catholics.

Many Christians see the successful spreading of the Gospel of Jesus Christ from Jerusalem to the ends of the earth as a demonstration of its divine power and authenticity, showing the positive impact of the faith on individuals of all cultures and the work of God's providence through history. Many Christians around the world are grateful to the missionaries who risked their lives to bring the Gospel to their countries and to translate the Bible into their languages. The result has frequently been new local churches led by indigenous peoples, worshipping using the music and art of their own cultures, no longer dependent on the countries which handed on the faith to them.

But many people in the West are now much less proud of Christianity and its reception around the world, looking back on the missionary successes of past centuries with awkwardness, embarrassment, or very deep shame. The history of Christian evangelism is interwoven with the history of colonialism and Western imperialism, in which missionaries travelled to remote lands alongside explorers, military forces and trading companies, bringing a complex mixture of benefits, hazards and tragedies. The era of European imperialism is now hugely controversial, with the cruelties of military conquest, slavery, commercial exploitation and racism deservedly facing criticism. Critics of the old imposition of Western authority and beliefs are widely found around the world. And those Westerners who are keen to look as if they have progressed beyond an intolerant past are often especially fierce in their criticism of Christian evangelism, which provides a very convenient scapegoat.

The re-evaluation of the Christian heritage of the West is part of a transition to pluralism and secularism which had been building up for a long time but which advanced especially rapidly during the second half of the twentieth century. It involved a steep decline in church attendance, a growth in the number of atheists and agnostics, rising numbers who described themselves as spiritual but not religious, and much immigration by members of other faiths from around the world.

In nations which used to regard themselves confidently as Christian, the Bible has mostly ceased to provide the shared worldview and language for public discussion of how life should be lived. With people of many different beliefs living side by side, there is now an assumption in most parts of the West that religion is largely a private matter and a minority interest.[164] It is pursued by individuals, extended families and ethnic subcultures in their own homes and places of worship, rather than being a set of objective truths that can be evaluated together. Trying to argue for or against any one religion in public may seem inappropriate, disrespectful or even dangerous. Many have been influenced by the postmodern theory that any attempt to spread a particular grand narrative about the meaning of life is a dangerous bid for power, out of place in a tolerant and diverse society.

Some now seek to enjoy the festivals, symbols and culinary traditions of many faiths and cultures while ignoring their truth claims, finding ways to share in the parties of Diwali, Eid al-Fitr and Hanukkah alongside Chinese New Year and Christmas. Meanwhile, some

---

164 The alliance between Republicans and Evangelicals in the United States which I described on
     p. 193 is an exception to this trend. American Protestantism retains a stronger sense that faith
     is a more public expression of group identity.

atheists campaign for the shared life of their nation to become even more explicitly secular.

Against this background, it now takes considerable bravery for Christians to attempt to persuade others of the truth of their faith. Those Christians who do seek to evangelise therefore tend to be the most zealous and the most conservative, and are sometimes not overly concerned with tact, diplomacy and sympathy for other perspectives. Often they get bogged down in arguments about women's ministry and same-sex relationships. Often they adopt a very confrontational approach, which can seem highly embarrassing to other Christians. But I think that a greater mistake is made by those who have abandoned the task of helping others to understand the Christian message. Their reticence may seem polite and appropriately deferential to the norms of today's society. But their lack of effort to engage with the world around them can cause their approach to Christianity to become very cliquey. Their churches may seem closed and confusing to any who have not grown up within them. That isolation fails to express the good news of reconciliation and forgiveness which Jesus sent from Jerusalem to the ends of the earth.

I will explore the strengths and weaknesses of the confrontational and cliquey approaches, and then suggest a way forward.

THE CONFRONTATIONAL APPROACH

The first confrontational Christians I encountered were some of the Evangelicals I met as an undergraduate, as I described in Chapter One. Freshers' Week at UK universities is famous as a very rare time when normal British social reserve is suspended, so that new students can strike up conversations with complete strangers. But my Freshers' Week included one conversation which was surprising even in that context, an unexpected encounter with a member of the Christian Union. She introduced herself when I was sitting on my own in the cafeteria, and quickly moved the conversation on to asking me if I believed in God. Having established that I had recently acquired some kind of faith, she eagerly sought further clarification about my beliefs by asking if I agreed that all human beings were evil and deserved to go to hell. She

said all of this with a warmth and enthusiasm which seemed oddly out
of keeping with her words, and was very keen to explain to me where I
was going wrong. This was not what I was expecting to experience all
of a sudden over lunch, even in Freshers' Week, but it was a memorable
part of the cascade of new experiences at university. I found her beliefs
quite strange, but she succeeded in showing me that there were people
around who would talk to me about faith whenever I wanted to, and
I did appreciate that. More of her Christian Union friends soon made
themselves known in the following weeks with a little more subtlety.

In their more aggressive forms, confrontational Christians are
widely regarded as a nuisance, or are thought to alienate more people
than they convince. People going about their daily lives do not often
rejoice when the Jehovah's Witnesses knock on the door, or the evangelist in the marketplace proclaims the imminent end of the world, or
the religious friend somehow steers yet another conversation around to
faith. Often these missionary enthusiasts focus on the precarious state
of their listener's souls, talking about divine judgement and the need
for individual salvation. Many conservative Christians diplomatically
avoid the controversies discussed in Chapters Five and Six, but some
seem to relish these additional opportunities to be counter-cultural.

The most confrontational of today's Christians tend to be the Evangelicals, who are confident that Christianity is uniquely true and that
they have a duty to preach the Gospel to the whole world without
exception. Particular groups may feel that they are being targeted and
judged, such as atheists, agnostics, Jews, liberal Christians, Catholics
or gay people, and sometimes that is the case. But the Evangelical message is that *all* have sinned and fallen short of the glory of God, and
will be saved if they put their faith in Jesus Christ.[165] Even the faithful
congregations of conservative churches often find themselves on the
receiving end of this preaching: their pastors take care to make sure
that everyone really has responded to Jesus with a genuine faith, rather
than just going through the motions of looking religious. Evangelical
Christians emphasise the uniqueness of Jesus Christ as the Son of God,

165 Romans 3.21-26; John 3.16

his crucifixion as the only means by which God's forgiveness reaches us, and the eternal significance of each individual's response to the Gospel.

Confrontational Christianity has various strengths and weaknesses. One positive feature is that it often involves a determined and honest attempt to make sense of things from one coherent religious perspective. It can be logical, consistent and clear. It can be held accountable to its own openly declared principles, such as its emphasis on the Bible and the central importance of Jesus Christ. It can also help to shape church communities which have a very clear sense of identity and shared purpose. Their members are often deeply committed and very generous with their time and money.

Another strength is that those who believe that salvation is only found through faith in Christ often work very hard to find ways of presenting their message clearly to the world, genuinely caring about the spiritual state of their friends and neighbours. Evangelicals often arrange their church services around the needs of visitors and new members, rather than around their own preferences. They take great care to offer a warm welcome to all, trying hard to communicate the faith very clearly to anyone who is interested. There is much genuine kindness and thoughtfulness in this way of running churches.

But there are also serious problems with confrontational Christianity. Firstly, it may simply be so strident that it scares people away. Any group which is very fierce in its judgements of outsiders is more likely to alienate them than to open up a fruitful conversation. And any group which is excessively earnest or desperate in its attempts to welcome people may start to seem like cultists or scammers who do not have others' best interests at heart. And any group which only forms friendships with non-Christians in the hope of converting them may cause those non-Christian friends to feel manipulated and deceived when they realise what is happening.

Secondly, there can be a dangerous failure to recognise ways in which there is genuine goodness, love and truth to be found amongst people of other beliefs. If a church is too fervent in its belief that everything outside its walls is darkness and depravity, it may be asking potential converts to repent of things which are actually good. For example, conservative Christians have often been too quick to dismiss the insights of secular philosophy, the experiences of loving relationships outside heterosexual marriage, the wisdom of other faiths, or the value of non-Christian literature, poetry, art and music. Requiring people to label goodness as evil and truth as falsehood leads to deep spiritual confusion, which can be very damaging.

Thirdly, confrontational Christianity needs to be extremely careful to avoid descending into something which is no more than basic human tribalism. Our default, unredeemed behaviour as social animals is to form ourselves into groups or gangs or factions, to seek status within our own teams, and to compete together against the other groups. This happens throughout all areas of human life, including the Church. Petty rivalry often blights the existence of politics and religion in all its forms and at all levels, from local parish councils to national political parties. We cheer on our own leaders, compete with each other to rise up the social hierarchy towards those leaders, and join forces in portraying the other groups as degenerate and dangerous. We may dress this rivalry up with all sorts of grand slogans about how we are the ones who believe in some great ideal, such as liberty, equality, progress, faith or the Bible, but often it amounts to little more than saying that our clan is better than your clan. Underneath the slogans, the social dynamics may not be very different from the ways that packs of wolves behave.

Christians engage in basic tribalism just as much as everyone else, idolising great preachers and pouring scorn on the 'false teachings' of those outside their particular group. If we do this, we have to keep asking ourselves whether we are really doing anything which goes beyond following some very basic and unredeemed social instincts.

The Gospels show that Jesus was very aware of this problem. He was hesitant even to be recognised as a leader of a new movement himself,[166] and said very little about how to run churches. Catholics like to think of him as the founder of a new institution, but he spoke about the reign of God on earth (the Kingdom of God) rather than drawing up the constitution of a new organisation of human beings. He frequently spent time with people who were considered outcasts by the

166 John 6.15

religious people of his time,[167] and his parables of judgement seem to undermine any attempt to draw a clear boundary between Christians and everyone else.[168] When offering an example of someone caring for his neighbour, he talked about a good Samaritan,[169] a figure regarded by his audience as a member of a false religion. Jesus put no time into describing how to build power bases and institutions, but focused on the need to receive the Kingdom of God humbly, like a little child, and said that true greatness was found in becoming the servant of all.[170]

Nevertheless, Jesus could still also be very confrontational. He said that he was himself the truth,[171] and he proclaimed the truth even when it put his own life in danger. He rebuked the powerful for their corruption and hypocrisy, and cleansed the Temple of those making money from the poor.[172] He sent his followers to risk their own lives in spreading his message around the world.[173] Those who are truly Christlike will not settle for the lazy tribalism that simply boasts that their group is the best, but they will still show a deep concern for truthfulness and justice. And they will still seek in love and vulnerability to communicate the message of the Gospel to the world, rather than holding onto it for their own comfort. Genuine Christianity will be alert to the dangers of confrontational tribalism, but can never abandon its vocation to pass on the message of Jesus Christ to others.

THE CLIQUEY APPROACH

In England and many other places, confrontational Christianity is rarer than the approach which completely avoids it, which I will call cliquey Christianity. When I began exploring faith, the Evangelicals went out of their way to give me a welcome which was very enthusiastic (sometimes a little too enthusiastic), but I found that most other groups were much harder to engage with.

167   Matthew 9.11
168   Matthew 25.31-46, Matthew 7.21-23
169   Luke 10:25-37
170   Mark 10.15; Mark 9.35
171   John 14.6
172   Mark 11.15
173   John 21.15-19

The problem is that nice, tolerant people react against the confrontational Christians and prefer to hide behind our society's reluctance to talk about religion. They remain instead in very private and inward-looking groups. With the excuse of not wanting to judge anyone for remaining outside the Church, they do very little to encourage anyone in. They end up giving the impression that the Church is only really there for those who grew up in it and who already understand it. And they resist displays of zealotry by becoming very vague about what they actually think about anything. Often they retreat entirely into the discussion of rotas, flower-arranging and picnics, perhaps also venturing out into the symbolic realms of poetry, music and art, leaving all the public debates about truth to the fervent atheists and the outspoken religious conservatives.

My most memorable encounter with a clique was a visit to a Greek Orthodox cathedral in England for their Easter service. The Orthodox celebrate Easter at a later date than other churches, so this seemed like an excellent opportunity for me to broaden my experience of denominations. I had just read a book on Orthodoxy from which I had learned that the Orthodox see themselves as the one true Church which Jesus Christ originally founded, regarding Protestants and Catholics as having departed from the truth. That claim seemed to demand my attention, so I assumed that those who believed it ought to feel something of a sense of responsibility. I expected that they should feel some kind of a call to explain themselves, some sense of a duty to the rest of the world to make known the truth which the creator of the universe had entrusted uniquely to them. But this was not at all evident.

When I arrived, everyone else obviously knew exactly what they were doing, having grown up with this form of Christianity. People were buying candles, lighting them and placing them in front of icons, bowing and crossing themselves, all absorbed in their own devotions. I hung around just inside the entrance looking as obviously lost as I could, hoping that someone might welcome me, but no one said anything. I searched in vain for any kind of service booklet or leaflet in any language. After being ignored for a long while, I went to speak to the man who was replenishing the stack of candles. I was new, I explained, and interested in Orthodoxy. Would there be a service booklet in English which I could borrow? He looked horrified. 'We are very busy!' he said. 'Come back another week.'

The service proceeded in ancient Greek, in which I recognised the occasional *Kyrie Eleison*, and involved much impressive drama and beauty. Clergy in elaborate robes occasionally appeared through doorways in a finely-painted screen and waved candles at the congregation. There was a time when people went forward to receive communion. My book had told me that I would not be allowed to do that, saying that there might be some unconsecrated bread for visitors which I would be able to receive instead. But there was no explanation or invitation concerning that, so I stayed rather awkwardly in my place.

Clearly, this was a home from home for Greek people in England. And at some level, many of them perhaps subscribed to the view that their religion was the closest thing to the truth to be found there. But they showed no sign at all that it might be their role to share the treasures of their faith with those seeking answers. It was hard to be sure about their attitude to visitors: at best it was indifference, but I was anxious that my presence as an outsider might have been actively annoying them.

Lest I sound too unfair to my Greek brothers and sisters, I should admit that this is simply one vivid example of a phenomenon I found in many other places. Middle-of-the-road Church of England churches are usually better than the Orthodox at having someone just inside the door who gives out service booklets and hymn books with a friendly greeting, but congregations can be quite embarrassed about actually talking to any newcomers. Catholics tend to assume that anyone attending Mass will have been taught exactly what to do when they were seven, so any service leaflets are usually incomplete and are baffling to the uninitiated. They rarely provide any explanation of what visitors are meant to do during the distribution of communion, even though this is strictly for Catholics only.

Most Christian cliques, perhaps unthinkingly, have capitulated to the current Western belief in pluralism, the assumption that all religions and philosophies can safely be treated as equally valid. Usually pluralism is not the official view of the denomination, as in my example of the Orthodox Church, but it is often the way that things work out in practice for ordinary churchgoers. It means that they regard their faith as something personal and private, something which is no one else's business and which they have no responsibility for sharing with anyone else.

Often they go as far as to believe in universalism, the expectation that God's love is so all-embracing and free from factional prejudice that all will inevitably go to heaven in the end somehow. Cliques therefore are much less likely to be concerned about the eternal state of anyone else's soul, and may be embarrassed or disturbed by any attempt to spread the Christian faith. They are much less likely to talk about the truth of Christian doctrine, and much more likely to talk about the beauties of Christian spirituality, enjoying the choirs and the candlelight while assuming that divine truth remains safely beyond all verbal definition and argument. Instead of telling others to repent and believe the Gospel, liberals with campaigning tendencies are more likely to team up with non-Christians who share a love of left-of-centre politics: seeking social justice, redistribution of wealth to the poor, and more urgent action to save the environment.

This pluralist, liberal, and often universalist approach sounds extremely warm, positive and socially responsible, but it tends to remove all sense of urgency about helping other people to explore the Christian faith. Without a sense that the local church has a duty to make everyone welcome, a congregation may simply become quite exclusive and snobbish, consisting of those who are proud of their very refined tastes in liturgy, spirituality, art and architecture. Or it may become a very niche group, representing one particular social or ethnic group or one generation, being rather frosty towards others. Most likely, it will be content to consist of those who were brought up in that kind of church, meaning that those from other backgrounds may always feel that they are outsiders or that they are making a failed attempt at social climbing. So a pluralist, liberal, universalist approach sounds very warm and affirming and rarely makes a nuisance of itself in public, but ironically often produces churches which feel closed and cliquey to others. Anyone who wants to explore the religion of a clique may need a lot of courage to find their way inside and may have an uphill struggle trying to make sense of it all. It can feel like trying to bluff one's way into a very exclusive golf club.

To my mind, a clique is failing in a basic Christian duty. If a church is not set up to welcome people in, to show them how Christian worship works and to help them to understand the Gospel without needing any previous knowledge, it is not living up to its calling. I also think that the underlying theological ideas of universalism and pluralism are not as helpful and responsible as they first seem.

STRENGTHS AND WEAKNESSES OF
PLURALISM AND UNIVERSALISM.

At first glance, a pluralist understanding of religious truth has much to commend it, since we enjoy the freedoms of living in a multicultural, diverse and pluralist society.[174] Part of being a good citizen today involves treating people of different beliefs with respect, warmth and generosity, learning to value and appreciate the riches of their various cultures and traditions. In that social sense, we should all be happy to relate to our world and our local communities in a pluralist way. But that social, neighbourly pluralism should not require us to abandon a sense that there might be such a thing as religious truth and that some religions might be closer to it than others.

Those who take a completely pluralist approach to their faith will insist that it is just one of many paths up the mountain to salvation or enlightenment, and that there are many other routes available which are somehow equally good and valid. They claim that all religions are in some (possibly very mysterious) sense the same. They like to think that, above the clash of contradictory ideas about gods, prophets, scriptures and saviours, there is some higher reality that all faiths all equally glimpse in their different ways. They therefore feel able to avoid any difficult discussions about how one approach to religion might be better than another.

174   The importance of freedom is a major theme in *The Theology of Everything* – see especially pp. 148-157

That is a very nice, well-intentioned thought, but it does not stand up to careful analysis. If I invent a new religion based around the Temple of the Holy Pineapple, whose one doctrine concerns the solemn drinking of fruit juice on Tuesday lunchtimes, this will not have the deep insights into human experience that can be found among Buddhists. The Heaven's Gate cult which organised a mass suicide in the belief that it would take them to a spacecraft following comet Hale-Bopp was completely and tragically deluded. Religious truth has not been shared out equally among all people and all faiths, nor is there some list of five or so great religions which have been proven be equally correct. Even those who like to think that they believe that all religions are equal may not be being honest with themselves: those who congratulate themselves on their tolerant pluralism are, for example, usually still rightly critical of religious groups which restrict the freedoms of women.

Pretending that all religions amount to the same thing is well-intentioned but inaccurate. It tends at best to lead to a shallow coexistence in which we can ignore each other and hide in our own shrines. This is better than having violent squabbles, but is a failure to relate deeply and openly to each other. A truly respectful and honest relationship between people of different faiths can include both celebrating common ground and also discussing interesting differences.

The most widespread pluralist view of religions is to say that religion is really all about learning to be good, learning to live a productive moral life alongside other people. It says that each religion has its myths, stories and parables to illustrate a moral life, along with various threats and promises to motivate people to be moral. It may sound at first as if this pluralist view is very affirming of all the faiths of the world. Actually, it involves heavily editing all faiths so that they can be forced to fit into a secular understanding of ethics, and is much less tolerant than it seems. Religions are all doing more than just expressing a set of values, and have interesting and important things to say about things like a relationship with God, the meaning of life, the nature of consciousness or the possibility of life beyond death. Pluralism risks losing sight of the distinctive and fascinating features of individual faiths by wrongly assuming that they are all the same.

A belief in universal salvation, similarly, seems to me to be less helpful than it appears on the surface.[175] It often begins with a very understandable reaction against some who have been too arrogant in proclaiming themselves as the only true believers and the only ones who will go to heaven. In response, a universalist vision of God reconciling the whole universe to himself seems much fairer. It allows the recognition of the goodness, love and truth which are found outside the boundaries of any religious faction. But can we really say that everyone is ultimately heading in the right direction? It is an attractive thought, but it seems like wishful thinking to me, not anchored in the teachings of Jesus or in our experiences of life.

Our choices and the beliefs that shape our lives have real consequences. There are many paths which lead to disaster and ruin rather than to God. There are people who are stuck in selfish, hateful and destructive approaches to life which are causing more and more problems for themselves and for those around them. There are people who have distorted some form of religion into a platform for violence or sexual exploitation. And there are people who despise the idea of being held accountable for their actions by any higher power. These and many other people are going the wrong way.

My view as a Christian is that life now is an opportunity to begin to grow into a relationship of love with God, a relationship that can continue after death. It seems to me that some people are doing that, and some people are not, although only God knows exactly where the boundary lies between those two groups. I think that this relationship is possible because of Jesus Christ, and I would seek to point everyone towards him. But I have met some people of other faiths who seem to me to be already closer to the true spirit of Christianity than most of those who call themselves Christians. And I have met some very wise and kindly atheists whose declared opposition to faith seems to me to owe more to some bad experiences of particular churches than to a rejection of who God really is. So I do not think that the boundary line around those who are getting to know God always lines up tidily

175 See Chapter Seven of *The Theology of Everything* for further discussion of Jesus' teachings about judgement, which seem to me to rule out universalism

with the membership of Christian churches. But I do think that there is
some kind of boundary. For example, there are some who would find
an everlasting life of worship to be a wonderful thing, and there are
some who would not. And I am not confident that people are likely to
be in the first group if they are not already exploring a life of prayer
and worship in some way here and now. The truth will emerge on the
Day of Judgement, when the true relationship between each person
and God will become clear.

But a belief that everyone will probably get to heaven in the end
troubles me in the same way as the belief that the environment will
probably be fine whatever we throw at it. I can see why it might feel
comforting, but it is actually quite lazy and irresponsible. Many people's answers really are wrong, and many people have an approach
to life which does not lead to the flourishing of themselves and others,
or to any kind of lasting relationship with God. And so I think it is a
serious failure when the Church ceases to articulate a coherent theology
and to make the message of the Gospel freely available to the world.
A lazy, cliquey pluralism and a naive universalism will not do. Much
of the clarity, generosity and engagement of the more confrontational
Christians is still needed.

A HEALTHY WAY FORWARD:
HOSPITALITY AND DIALOGUE

Avoiding the problems of confrontations and cliques, a better way forward is one of friendly engagement. This involves generous hospitality
and an openness to real discussion, without ever taking offence and
without avoiding difficult questions. I think that 1 Peter 3.15 is very
significant:

> Always be ready to make your defence to anyone who
> demands from you an accounting for the hope that is in you;
> yet do it with gentleness and reverence.

I am deeply grateful to many Christian friends, to the dean and
chaplain of the college where I was an undergraduate, to the minister
of the first church I joined, and to all those who went out of their way

to be hospitable. They made me feel at home in their services, ensured that I was not left feeling isolated and foolish, answered my questions, and helped me find my way into the Christian faith. I owe a lot to the congregations of all the churches I visited when exploring that faith who greeted me warmly, handed me all the necessary books and booklets needed to follow the service, helped me to find a place to sit, chatted to me afterwards if I lingered and wanted to talk, or let me slip away quietly if that was what I felt like doing.

As a chaplain today, I try to run a chapel in a way which is open and hospitable, with a clear intellectual core that is there for those who are interested in exploring it. I invite everyone to engage with us at any level they choose. This means running social events which make people feel welcome in the Chapel. It means being very accepting of those who would say that they are only there for the music or out of interest in history and tradition. It means helping them to feel comfortable: showing them to seats if they are looking lost, making sure that there are clear service sheets and helpful instructions so that everyone knows what is going on. If there is communion, no one should feel awkward or embarrassed or under any kind of pressure at that point, but everyone should understand how things work if they wish to take communion, receive a blessing, or remain quietly in their seats.

Meanwhile, I run talks and Bible studies every week, showing that there is a clear content to the Christian faith which is there for people to explore and to engage with. And I make it clear that I am there to respond to all of their questions and to help them find answers. I show that there is a journey towards baptism and confirmation if they wish it, and onwards to various kinds of responsibility in the running of the Chapel, and for some towards an exploration of vocation to Christian ministry.

Hospitality, a clearly-stated theology, and a willingness to explain the Christian faith to all who are interested are vitally important. The vagueness of pluralism sounds tolerant at first, but can actually be evasive and unfriendly. It is much easier to form relationships and to think deeply about things that matter when people learn how to be gentle but honest. I have learned in my ministry that people find my talks much more interesting and helpful if I set out a clear position and explain it than if I politely avoid saying anything definite. It is perfectly possible to outline a belief with precision while also treating others with respect if they disagree with it. And they find it much more useful when they can use my ideas as a landmark, a way of getting their bearings, even if they then take up a position which is somewhat different.

We are missing out on so much if we do not cultivate these kinds of conversations. If we leave discussions about truth to the angry extremists, then we may reassure others that we are harmless, but we may also give them the impression that our beliefs have no intellectual substance or credibility. They may assume that our faith is obviously irrational, like a childish belief in Father Christmas or the Tooth Fairy.

But, as I have argued here and in *The Theology of Everything*, there is an approach to Christianity which can be explained clearly, rationally, drawing on all of our human experiences of the world, pulling in all the data we can from all of our senses and faculties, and engaging with the testimonies to the work of God which we find in Scripture and tradition. All of that can be shared, with no need for confrontations or threats or special pleading or taking offence or attempting to seize power, and no need to withdraw into eccentric cliques.

This model of friendly presence, hospitality, and readiness to discuss the truth is one which is found very clearly in the Church of England's historic patterns of ministry. The parish system placed an educated Christian minister in a very visible position at the heart of every community, presenting a clear identity and also seeking to be available to care for everyone. This system is under very great pressure at the moment, creaking under the strain of maintaining historic buildings with dwindling congregations. But there are many wonderful people who still keep it going, and they are doing something incredibly valuable.

In recent times, the Alpha Course and other programmes like it have often been very successfully hospitable. Alpha Courses are sometimes distorted by over-zealously confrontational Christians, but when run as intended they provide an excellent combination of good food, very focused talks and very open discussions. Even just the step of setting up a course sends a powerful message that the church is there to welcome newcomers, rather than existing only for those who already understand how everything works.

It is useful also to counteract the widely-held perception that religious people are characterised by being very quick to take offence. I find that people are endlessly amazed when they discover that they really can ask me anything about theology, and that I will not be upset by their doubts, or disappointed by their ignorance, or outraged at their different views. Instead, I am always pleased when I come across those who are curious about faith. It is a huge privilege to be able to be hospitable and to support them in their journey.

This approach of having a clear identity and engaging hospitably with others can fit well with a more accurate view of the human condition. Confrontational Christians often assume that the world is in total spiritual darkness outside their own correct kind of faith, while cliquey Christians often assume that everyone can safely be left to find their own kind of light somehow. But the truth is that the world is a complex mixture of good and evil, of integrity and corruption, of truth and falsehood, in a way which does not line up with the boundaries of any institution or faction. Truth and error exist and must be taken seriously (as the conservative Christians know), but the truth is not confined entirely to one group (as the pluralists know). Evil may lurk within our own much-loved walls. Goodness, beauty and truth may be glimpsed and communicated even by those we most distrust. Jesus said that he was the light of the world, the light that enlightens all people,[176] not just the light of the Church. The Holy Spirit is at work in more ways than we could ever know, and there are many encounters with God which do not fit tidily into a Christian framework of scripture and sacrament. Christians who are hospitable to non-Christians can often see something of Christ in them.

Christians can best enter into dialogue with people of other beliefs by cultivating both humility and generosity. The humility means listening deeply and being willing to learn, open to discovering the ways that God has gone ahead of us. And the generosity means avoiding

176 John 8.12, John 1.1

cliquey laziness by making the effort to articulate a clear understanding of Christianity in a way which others can grasp. Christians have important stories to tell: both of Jesus Christ himself, and of our own deepest experiences and journeys of faith.

This approach involves vulnerability: we may be challenged by what we learn from other people, and by our encounters with others; and we may feel very open to ridicule or criticism when we reveal the truths and events which have shaped us most deeply. But this vulnerability is the way of Jesus Christ, the way of the cross. Instead of hiding in groups of the like-minded, the Church is called to share in his work of reconciliation. It is an act of great kindness when we reach out across our tribal divisions, showing the ability to talk honestly, warmly, openly and truthfully about the things that really matter.

CONCLUSION

In Chapter Five, I argued for a view of women's leadership which engages deeply with important themes in the Scriptures while looking seriously at historical context. I described a middle way between the shallow verse-quoting of many conservative Christians and the tendency of many liberal Christians to dismiss the Bible as irrelevant in this area. I took a similar approach in Chapter Six, arguing that the affirmation of same-sex relationships is compatible with the ways in which good theology has developed in the past, continuing a process of taking both Scripture and context seriously.

In this final chapter, I have argued that the Church has a duty to make people welcome and to explain the Christian faith. It is not enough to embrace the liberal and universalist hope that everyone will somehow find heaven on whichever path they follow through life.

Here again, a central approach can build on the strengths of both sides and avoid their errors. On the one hand, conservatives who work hard at evangelism often undermine their message by insisting that women cannot be leaders or that gay people must all be celibate. Their message is clear and confident, but it loses credibility through their failure to recognise the goodness that can exist outside of their traditional rules. A lack of concern for environmental issues[177] often makes this worse, convincing many of their hearers that Christianity has little to do with any real sense of what is right and true.

On the other hand, liberals often do not bother with any kind of attempt to communicate the distinctive features of their faith. They may campaign on the issues of equality for women, same-sex marriage and environmental concern, but they usually do so in a way which blends in with secular approaches. They may hope that their churches will attract new members by making progress in social justice, but the evidence is mostly that liberal churches decline when they are unable to explain how Christianity has any unique point to it.

From the centre, it is possible to have a confident theology which can be explained in a book like this. It does not need to be nervous, muddled or politely reticent, but it can be offered confidently to the world. It can draw on all the strengths of the various parts of the Church, while rejecting their errors. It can be a theology which engages both with the Scriptures and with the opportunities and challenges brought by developments in society. It can thereby invite all people to encounter the grace of God for themselves.

From the centre, there can be a clear Christian message which does affirm the ordination of women and the blessing of same-sex couples, while also faithfully communicating the distinctive good news of the relationship with God made possible by the death and resurrection of Jesus, as revealed in the Scriptures.

From the centre, all of the riches of Christian spirituality and liturgy developed over the centuries can be explored and enjoyed. For all who get involved, God's great work of reconciliation enables a life of prayer and worship in the power of the Holy Spirit which leads onwards to the joys of the world to come.

177 A theme I tackled in *The Theology of Everything*, pp. 51-60

SUGGESTIONS FOR FURTHER READING

For a popular presentation of the idea that God's love will ultimately save all people, see *Love Wins* by Rob Bell (2012, Collins).

By contrast, C. S. Lewis powerfully argues that God respects the choices that we make for or against him, found especially in *The Great Divorce* (2012, Collins).

The content of the *Alpha Course* is found in *Questions of Life* by Nicky Gumbel (2018, Hodder and Stoughton), and the details of how to run a course are in *Telling Others: The Alpha Initiative* (2018, Hodder and Stoughton). Alpha has a charismatic Evangelical theology, but has been used by over 24 million people around the world in Protestant and Catholic churches of many kinds, some of whom unofficially adapt it to reduce the emphasis on the miraculous work of the Holy Spirit or to add in their own perspectives.

There are many less well known alternatives. *Christianity Explored* by Rico Tice (2002, Authentic Lifestyle) takes a more conservative Evangelical approach, giving a greater emphasis on sin and judgement. The *Emmaus Course* brings in some Anglo-Catholic perspectives and is designed to be broadly accepted across the middle ground of the Church of England: the main volume is *Emmaus: Nurture* by Stephen Cottrell and Steven Croft (2010, Church House Publishing).

All of these courses may move too quickly to convince a sceptical atheist. My own book on *The Theology of Everything* (2017, Ellis and Maultby), which derives partly from my conversations with students, aims to show the ways in which a belief in God can help to make sense of all our areas of knowledge and experience.

Combined Index

The View from the Centre functions partly as a companion volume to my first book, *The Theology of Everything* (see details on page 237). In *The Theology of Everything*, I looked at how Christian faith can make sense of all areas of human knowledge and experience in one big picture, which included looking at central Christian doctrines about creation, Jesus, the atonement, and life after death. I have tried to avoid too much repetition, so *The View from the Centre* moves swiftly through some important areas which are tackled in more detail in the first book.

Since *The Theology of Everything* was published without an index, it seems useful to take this opportunity to produce a combined index to both books.

'VC' indicates *The View from the Centre*, while 'TE' indicates *The Theology of Everything*. Headings are in italics when the subject only appears in *The Theology of Everything*.

VC: pages in this book
TE: pages in *The Theology of Everything*

VC: pages in this book
TE: pages in *The Theology of Everything*

VC: pages in this book
TE: pages in *The Theology of Everything*

VC: pages in this book
TE: pages in The Theology of Everything

VC: pages in this book
TE: pages in *The Theology of Everything*

ALSO BY KEITH EYEONS:
THE THEOLOGY OF EVERYTHING

Human beings have gathered a vast amount of knowledge, but we each know only a little of it. We become specialists in narrow fields, from Airbus pilots to Zulu historians, then find it difficult to see what all of these areas of expertise might mean together.

This book makes two radical claims. The first is that all of our human faculties have evolved to show us important things about the universe, including our appreciation of beauty, our ability to make scientific measurements, our awareness of meaning and goodness, and our experiences of consciousness and community. We usually divide these different kinds of insights among different professions, but we can gain a far deeper understanding of reality if we bring them all together. The second claim is that it is Christian theology which can reveal that unity, resuming a traditional role that it has largely abandoned in recent centuries.

Far more comprehensively than atheism, a belief in God can offer a framework which makes sense of all our experiences in one coherent, rational and inspiring picture, a true theory of everything.

The Theology of Everything was shortlisted for the 2019 Michael Ramsey Prize, which celebrates the most promising contemporary theological writing from the global Church.

'A wonderful book that weaves theology, philosophy and science to help us think deeply about the life and faith of Christians in the world today. A must-read.'

Justin Welby, Archbishop of Canterbury

'Highly accessible, admirably clear and with an ambitious arc to match its title, this book sweeps up and over the frames within which others have often tried to understand the world and lands on its own theology of everything. I wish I'd read it years ago.'

Loretta Minghella, First Church Estates Commissioner

'The Theology of Everything challenges the cultural narratives of power and control on the one hand and purposelessness on the other. Instead, it offers a third way in which God draws us into freedom, community and compassion. Let it challenge you as to how we fit into the bigger picture of the universe.'

Sarah Mullally, Bishop of London